ROBERT MUGABE'S

ZIMBABWE

JAMES R. ARNOLD

ROBERTA WIENER

 TWENTY-FIRST CENTURY BOOKS　**MINNEAPOLIS**

Twenty-First Century Books
A division of Lerner Publishing Group, Inc.
241 First Avenue North
Minneapolis, MN 55401 U.S.A.

Website address: www.lernerbooks.com

Library of Congress Cataloging-in-Publication Data

Arnold, James R.
    Robert Mugabe's Zimbabwe / by James R. Arnold and Roberta
Wiener.
       p.   cm. — (Dictatorships)
    Includes bibliographical references and index.
    ISBN 978–0–8225–7283–1 (lib. bdg. : alk. paper)
    1. Mugabe, Robert Gabriel, 1924– 2. Zimbabwe—Politics and
government—1980– 3. Presidents—Zimbabwe—Biography. I. Wiener,
Roberta, 1952– II. Title.
DT3000.A75 2008
968.9105'1—dc22   2006100765

Manufactured in the United States of America
1 2 3 4 5 6 – DP – 13 12 11 10 09 08

CONTENTS

INTRODUCTION: INDEPENDENCE DAY PROMISES 6

CHAPTER 1: ZIMBABWE'S PAST 12

CHAPTER 2: THE MAKING OF AN
AFRICAN NATIONALIST 32

CHAPTER 3: MUGABE'S VICTORY 40

CHAPTER 4: MUGABE'S REGIME:
DATELINE TO DESPOTISM 54

CHAPTER 5: INSTITUTIONS UNDER ATTACK 86

CHAPTER 6: TOOLS OF A DICTATOR 96

CHAPTER 7: LIVING IN MUGABE'S ZIMBABWE 110

CONCLUSTION: AFTER MUGABE 134

WHO'S WHO? 140

TIMELINE 146

GLOSSARY 148

BIBLIOGRAPHY 151

FURTHER READING, WEBSITES, AND BLOGS . . .152

SOURCE NOTES 154

INDEX 158

JUST BEFORE MIDNIGHT ON APRIL 17, 1980, forty thousand excited spectators packed a soccer stadium in Zimbabwe's capital city to witness an astonishing sight. An honor guard of one hundred white soldiers and black soldiers marched into the stadium and presented arms. Just four months earlier, these soldiers had opposed each other in a long and bloody guerrilla war between Rhodesia's minority white supremacist government and African nationalists and their supporters. With peace at hand, soldiers lowered the British flag representing Rhodesia's history as one of Britain's African colonies. They replaced it with the flag of the newly independent and newly named Republic of Zimbabwe.

The nation's elected leader, a black nationalist named Robert Gabriel Mugabe, expressed his gratitude for inheriting a jewel, a country with one of the most productive agricultures in all of

SOLDIERS RAISE THE FLAG OF
Zimbabwe on April 17, 1980. The
ceremony marked a shift in power in
the southeastern African country.

Africa. He said that he would work with whites and blacks alike to maintain this jewel. Standing before a crowd of dignitaries from around the world, Mugabe was sworn in as Zimbabwe's first prime minister.

In 2005 Zimbabwe celebrated its twenty-fifth anniversary of independence. Mugabe had run the country for all of that time. During his tenure, Mugabe had betrayed his

MUGABE *(CENTER)* **SPEAKS TO REPORTERS DURING HIS FIRST PRESS**
conference after winning the 1980 election. At the time, many people were optimistic about Zimbabwe's chances to stabilize and prosper.

original promise and established instead a dictatorship based on terror. Human rights organizations worldwide severely criticized Mugabe's record.

Yet in 2005, the eighty-one-year-old Mugabe seemed ready to ignore such criticism. He again showed his ability to stir the passions of black nationalism, delivering a powerful address to his nation that inspired those loyal to him: "Twenty-five years have gone by since that eventful midnight of 17 April 1980 when our country was born, proudly taking up her place among members of the community of nations as a full, independent and sovereign state. This birth followed bitter struggles and wars of resistance waged by our people for nearly a century, struggles meant to dislodge British settler colonialism."

He went on to speak about the difficult fight to overthrow white rule and eloquently explained the importance of equitable redistribution of land, a process of land reform he claimed was complete. "Land . . . is a symbol of sovereignty, it is the economy, indeed, the source of our welfare as Africans. It remains the core social question of our time, as indeed, it was the main grievance on which our liberation struggle was based."

However, land reform in Zimbabwe was far from complete. Mugabe had driven white farmers off their land and replaced them with people loyal to his regime. But many of these replacements knew nothing about farming. Consequently, the Zimbabwean economy—based largely on agriculture—had declined disastrously. Where once Zimbabwe had served as the breadbasket (a major food-producing region) of southern Africa, the country now had to import food to feed its people. In addition, Zimbabwe's educational

AGRICULTURE HAS LONG BEEN THE MAIN SOURCE OF INCOME FOR PEOPLE in Zimbabwe. These workers are carrying crops of tea to market in the 1950s.

system was in tatters, with some 300,000 children forced to leave school because their parents could not afford to pay tuition. The nation's health care system was also in terrible shape, overwhelmed by a pandemic of AIDS, a lack of skilled care providers, and a lack of money to purchase medicine. Mugabe spoke about laying the "foundation" for economic growth. However, later in the year he would launch a military attack on his own people, evicting hundreds of thousands of urban poor and destroying their homes and work-places. Throughout the country, only Mugabe's loyalists enjoyed a prosperous and healthy life.

Mugabe ended his address to the nation by returning to a favorite theme: his role in overthrowing oppressive white rule and creating an independent Zimbabwe. He concluded with the rousing cry, "Africa for Africans." Yet, for all the hopeful promises, Robert Gabriel Mugabe has traveled an incredible and tragic path from inspiring black nationalist leader to one of the world's most feared and corrupt dictators.

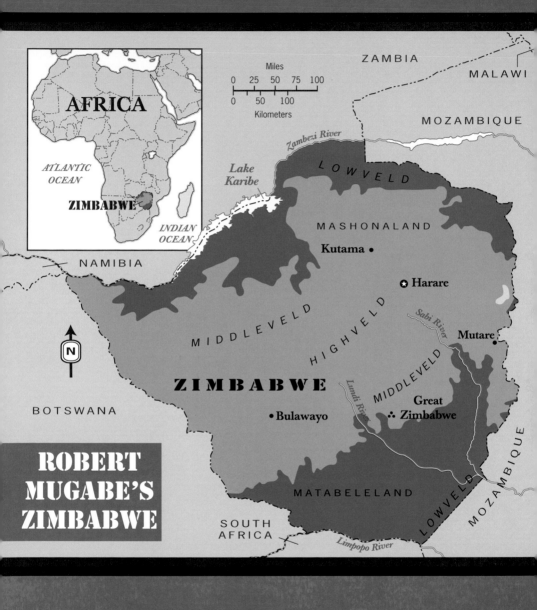

ROBERT
MUGABE'S
ZIMBABWE

ZIMBABWE IS A LANDLOCKED NATION IN SOUTHEASTERN AFRICA with a history that goes back thousands of years. With a land area of 150,873 square miles (390,761 square kilometers), it is slightly smaller than California. It is bordered on the south by the Limpopo River, which separates Zimbabwe from South Africa. Botswana lies on Zimbabwe's southwest and western border. The Zambezi River is the northern boundary between Zimbabwe and Zambia. Zimbabwe's eastern border is shared with Mozambique.

The earliest known people to live in Zimbabwe were called the Bushmen, or San. They lived a nomadic life of hunting and gathering for thousands of years before recorded history. The Shona people entered this land from the north about one thousand years ago, bringing their cattle with them. They pushed out the San and settled the land as farmers, raising cattle and planting crops. The early

MOST OF THE GREAT ZIMBABWE WAS BUILT IN THE FOURTEENTH AND fifteenth centuries, using stone but no mortar. The outer wall of its great enclosure is more than 800 feet (244 meters) long.

Shona also built the fortress known as the Great Zimbabwe. This fortress became the center of a kingdom, but the kingdom collapsed and the fortress was abandoned.

Meanwhile, to the south of Zimbabwe lived Mzilikazi, a former commander in the army of the great Shaka, king of the Zulu nation of

Zululand. Mzilikazi feuded with Shaka and fled Zululand around 1828. Mzilikazi and his followers moved northward, conquering smaller tribes on the way. Around 1837 the Boers (Dutch colonists of South Africa) drove him and about ten thousand of his people across the Limpopo River into present-day Zimbabwe. Mzilikazi founded the Ndebele kingdom near present-day Bulawayo around 1840.

Rivalry between the two largest segments of the population, the Shona and the Ndebele, played a major role in Zimbabwean history. Both groups speak Bantu languages—the Shona speak Mashona, and the Ndebele speak Sindebele. The Shona dominated Zimbabwe until the 1830s, when the Ndebele appeared on their border. The Ndebele spent the next fifty years slaughtering the

THE COMING OF MISSIONARIES, SUCH AS THE GROUP SHOWN ABOVE, IN
the nineteenth century started the wave of white settlers in Zimbabwe.

Shona, stealing their cattle, and establishing themselves as the dominant people of Zimbabwe. Thereafter, an uneasy peace between the tribes took hold.

When the Ndebele leader Mzilikazi allowed a British missionary (religious teacher) to enter and live in his territory in the late 1850s, he could not have known that he was admitting the first of his people's conquerors. Mzilikazi died in 1868, and—after a power struggle—his son, Lobengula, became the ruler of the Ndebele.

THE COMING OF THE EUROPEANS

During the Age of Exploration (early 1400s to early 1600s), European navigators searched for a trade route to connect Europe with India. This effort led Christopher Columbus to sail west across the Atlantic Ocean, where he accidentally discovered the New World in 1492. However, before Columbus, Portuguese sailors had begun sailing south from Portugal along the western coast of Africa. They gradually acquired enough knowledge to sail around the southern tip of Africa and continue north, up Africa's east coast. By the end of the fifteenth century, they wanted to explore Africa's interior in hopes of finding a way to connect their settlements on the west coast with their new discoveries along the east coast. The first European to set foot in what later became Zimbabwe was Portuguese explorer Antonio Fernandes, in 1511.

As time passed, European nations competed to colonize Africa. The competition continued through the end of the nineteenth century as the Age of Exploration gave way to the Age of Imperialism (1850–1914). The imperial powers—Great Britain, Germany, France, Italy, Belgium, and Portugal—eventually carved up the African continent. Their goal was to exploit Africa's wealth, particularly its natural resources, which included diamonds, gold, land, and cattle. In pursuit of economic gain, a small number of white Europeans settled in Africa. Backed by the power of their national governments, particularly their armies and navies, the white minority came to dominate the continent's black majority.

Zimbabwe ultimately fell under British domination. Wealthy diamond trader Cecil John Rhodes of Great Britain founded the British South Africa Company in 1889. Rhodes planned to build a railroad running the length of Africa. As was typical of European imperialism, Britain's Queen Victoria granted Rhodes and his company sweeping authority to enter African territory, place it under British "protection," and govern it as he saw fit.

The majority of Europeans thought it perfectly moral to occupy African lands and to manage the people living there. They justified this behavior on several grounds. The Europeans claimed they were helping to improve the lives of Africans—whom they viewed as "savages"—by making

CECIL JOHN RHODES WAS AN ardent colonialist who believed African countries would be better off under the rule of Great Britain.

the land more productive. They also claimed they were showing the Africans the path to the true God. To this end, various Christian denominations established missions to teach their religion to the Africans. In fact, Robert Mugabe was born at a Jesuit mission in 1924 and received his early education there.

KING LOBENGULA *(CENTER)* **WAS THE** last king of the Ndebele people. He reigned from 1870 to 1894.

The British South Africa Company claimed the regions that came to be called Northern Rhodesia and Southern Rhodesia (modern-day Zimbabwe). In 1888 Charles Rudd (one of Rhodes's employees) persuaded King Lobengula of the Ndebele to grant the so-called Rudd Concession. The Rudd Concession allowed the British South Africa Company to set up mining operations in a designated area in the king's territory of Matabeleland, in Southern Rhodesia. King Lobengula later changed his mind and tried to regain control of Matabeleland. His attempt failed, and the company insisted that the king had granted them rights not only in Matabeleland, but in Mashonaland as well. Furthermore, although the Rudd Concession had granted the British South Africa Company the right to extract minerals only, the company interpreted the agreement to include the right to take land and settle on it.

THE PIONEER COLUMN

The British South Africa Company's first move, in 1890, was to organize the Pioneer Column, a group of white soldiers and settlers drawn from the British inhabitants of neighboring South Africa. It aimed to gain control of Mashonaland and make it safe for white settlement. The black African inhabitants, for their part, did not conceive of land as something that could be bought, sold, or owned. Rather, they saw it as a shared resource, like air or water.

The Pioneer Column consisted of about one thousand young men from influential families. Each recruit was promised a mining claim plus 3,000 acres (1,215 hectares) of land. The men built a fort on the site that eventually became the capital city of Salisbury (renamed Harare when Zimbabwe gained independence). By the end of September 1890, these men began staking their claims to the land they had been promised.

The white settlers found a land that possessed extraordinary scenic beauty, good farmland, and the promise of gold and mineral deposits. Their favorable reports attracted more settlers. Most came from Great Britain, but others emigrated from France, Portugal, Greece, and South Africa. The growing white population claimed ever more land and mining rights. They also maneuvered the Shona population into providing cheap labor. The British South Africa Company accomplished this initially by taxing the huts in which the Shonas lived, thus forcing Shona men to work for the money to pay the tax.

The military force organized as part of the Pioneer Column evolved into the police force of Rhodesia, called the British South Africa Police. In 1980, the year Zimbabwe gained independence, it was renamed the Zimbabwe Republic Police and included blacks.

The company also resorted to force, rounding up the men at gunpoint and marching them off to work in the mines it had established.

The initial reports about the ease of life in Rhodesia proved misleading. The pioneers struggled during the early years, beset by drought and crop failure. They found that the gold deposits were not as substantial as expected. Their solution was to acquire more land, so they began looking for a chance to fight the Ndebele and drive them away. The chance came in 1893. Ndebele warriors attacked a Shona village. The Shona fled to a white-held fort. The Ndebele demanded that the whites surrender the Shona. The whites refused and fighting began. The whites possessed modern weapons against which the Ndebele warriors could not compete. This Matabele War ended with the Ndebele defeated and King Lobengula forced to flee. Lobengula died in exile in 1894. Having defeated the Ndebele, the company divided up the Ndebele's land and cattle. They claimed the most fertile and best-watered land of the region's cooler highlands, called the Highveld, leaving both the Ndebele and the Shona with the drier lowlands, called the Lowveld.

REBELLION:
THE FIRST CHIMURENGA

In 1896 the Ndebele and the Shona joined forces in a desperate attempt to eject the whites in a war called the First Chimurenga (war of liberation). About 400 whites, mostly settlers, died in the war. The whites viewed the war as unprovoked savagery by the Ndebele and the Shona. The blacks viewed it as a fight for their homeland and their survival. Cecil Rhodes personally persuaded the Ndebele chiefs to make peace. Sporadic fighting against the Shona continued into 1897. By the end of the year, the British South Africa Company had suppressed all armed resistance by the Shona and the Ndebele and hanged their leaders. The victorious British forced the Ndebele and the Shona to coexist, but the Shona's resentment of the Ndebele's hostile entry into their ancestral lands eventually affected twentieth-century politics.

The conflict had broken the Ndebele. In addition to their human losses, the Ndebele's cattle herds, the major source of their wealth, had been reduced by disease and plunder (the taking of goods by force). The white settlers then continued on their course of disrupting traditional African life and subjugating the population.

COLONIAL LIFE

The colony was named Southern Rhodesia in Rhodes's honor, and the British South Africa Company continued to govern it as a British protectorate until 1923. Almost from the time the first whites settled in Rhodesia, they sought self-government. In 1922 the thirty-four thousand white voters chose to make Southern Rhodesia a separate British colony rather than join the Union of South Africa. The following year, Southern Rhodesia became a self-governing British Crown Colony. Great Britain retained control of external affairs and had the final say regarding legislation that directly affected blacks. However, the company founded by Cecil Rhodes continued to dominate politics and business for many years.

The British prime minister's policy was to follow Rhodes's wish to build a Rhodesian society of "equal rights for all civilized men." While on the surface this sounded fair, the laws put in place by the whites ensured that few blacks would be considered "civilized." The colonial government imposed complete racial

THE COLONIAL GOVERNMENT IMPOSED SEGREGATION IN SCHOOLS, SUCH as this one for black children, throughout the middle of the twentieth century.

segregation of housing, schools, and hospitals. Southern Rhodesia's constitution provided for an all-white Parliament and required that voters be British citizens and meet a minimum income level. This effectively denied most blacks the right to vote. Some time in the future, white leaders said, blacks would be given political power. But first they had to become wiser and more experienced. According to the white leaders, if blacks were given political power too soon, they would not know how to use it effectively. They would undo all the economic gains that had followed the arrival of the whites.

Indeed, the new Crown Colony of Southern Rhodesia enjoyed economic growth based on agriculture and mining. But the benefits were not shared equally among whites and blacks. White farmers owned the best agricultural land, and white Britons wielded absolute power over the black majority. Comprising only about 4 percent of the population, whites earned 60 percent of the income. White households had incomes averaging ten times higher than the average black household income. Whites of all classes enjoyed greater wealth and leisure than they ever could have hoped for in England.

A series of land distribution laws unequally assigned the nation's land between blacks and whites. Nearly one million black people received 40,000,000 acres (16,200,000 hectares) of low-quality land, while forty thousand whites were given 49,000,000 highly fertile acres (19,800,000 hectares). The government created Native Reserves, later called Tribal Trust Lands. These arid plots were the only places where Africans could attempt to eke a living from the land. In the cities, blacks could live only in all-black townships. Blacks could not buy homes or land in white areas, nor could whites buy homes or land in black areas.

WHITE RHODESIANS WERE PART OF THE ELITE IN SOUTHERN RHODESIA.

They enjoyed greater wealth and privileges, but as black unrest grew, many whites found it necessary to arm themselves for protection.

THE RISE OF AFRICAN NATIONALISM

In 1941 U.S. president Franklin D. Roosevelt met with British prime minister Winston Churchill. Roosevelt disliked British imperialism. He pressured Churchill to issue the Atlantic Charter. The charter stated that the United States and Great Britain "respect the right of all peoples to choose the form of government under which they will live; and they wish to see sovereign rights and self-government restored to those who have been forcibly deprived of them." Around the world, nationalists took note of this ringing endorsement for self-rule.

RHODESIAN LAWS

The white rulers of Rhodesia had the power to organize life however they pleased, so they formulated laws for their own benefit. Their laws gave whites the best land, curtailed the rights of black people, and protected government authority by making it illegal for government opponents to engage in political activity. Here are some examples of those laws:

1898: Southern Rhodesia Native Regulations require all Africans to register and carry passes.

1930: Land Apportionment Act establishes Native Reserves for blacks, while giving all other land to whites.

1934: A labor law bars black Africans from working at skilled trades or living in white areas of towns and cities. Blacks can enter cities only as menial or domestic employees. Strikes are banned.

1951: Native Land Husbandry Act allocates small plots of pastureland to black Africans, which forces them to reduce their cattle herds, and prohibits urban black employees from owning rural land.

1959: Native Affairs Amendment Act bans unapproved meetings, assemblies, and political activity among black Africans; Preventive Detention Act permits any person to be detained for any reason; Unlawful Organizations Act bans the African National Congress (ANC) and similar political organizations working for majority rule.

1960: Law and Order Maintenance Act outlaws political speech and activity in opposition to the government. (Mugabe still uses this law against his opponents.)

1969: Land Tenure Act divides the land in half between the races, with the minority white population getting the better half.

After the end of World War II (1939–1945), American political leaders continued to pressure the British and other European colonial powers to grant independence to their colonies. Western sentiment began to turn against the injustice of wealthy Western nations running colonies for their own benefit. Westerners began to see the unfairness of a small white minority ruling a powerless black majority. At the same time, many Africans had seen the wider world while helping their European colonizers to fight the war. Many more had obtained educations and begun to question their colonial status. The desire for independence took root and grew among a new generation of black Africans.

In Southern Rhodesia, blacks formed political organizations in an effort to obtain fair representation. Meanwhile, Great Britain began to grant independence to its African colonies with the expectation that the black majority would take over the government of each nation. Uganda became independent in 1962; Kenya in 1963; and neighboring Zambia and Malawi in 1964. Britain expected Southern Rhodesia to convert to majority rule as a condition of independence, but the minority white population did not want to give up its power to the black majority. Many white Rhodesians believed the Africans to be an inferior people incapable of self-government.

Southern Rhodesia's government had made a minor concession in 1961, permitting blacks to hold fifteen of the sixty-five parliamentary seats. However, in 1964, a white supremacist party, the Rhodesian Front, won the national election, elevating Ian Smith to the office of prime minister. When Great Britain refused to grant independence to Southern Rhodesia's racist regime, Smith's government illegally enacted the Unilateral Declaration of Independence on November 11, 1965, creating the white-controlled, independent nation of Rhodesia. This decision marked the first time since the American Revolution (1776–1783) that a British colony had rebelled against its government.

THE SECOND CHIMURENGA

Great Britain would not use force to reverse Rhodesia's defiant declaration of independence. However, the international community refused to recognize Rhodesian independence.

AFRICAN INDEPENDENCE

Great Britain, France, Germany, Belgium, Portugal, Spain, and Italy all had a colonial foothold in Africa at one time or another. South Africa became an independent nation in 1910, ruled by the white descendants of European settlers. Germany lost its African colonies to the victors of World War I (1914–1918). Only Ethiopia maintained its independence, except for a brief period of Italian occupation.

Great Britain's influence extended over at least twelve African colonies or protectorates. These colonies or protectorates included Bechuanaland (present-day Botswana), Gold Coast (present-day Ghana), Kenya, Nigeria, Northern Rhodesia (present-day Zambia), Nyasaland (present-day Malawi), Sierra Leone, Southern Rhodesia (present-day Zimbabwe), Sudan, Tanzania, and Uganda.

Great Britain withdrew from Egypt in 1947 and Sudan in 1956. Also in 1956, France granted independence to Tunisia and Morocco. Algeria

PRIME MINISTER IAN SMITH HOLDS A PRESS CONFERENCE IN OCTOBER
1965. One month later, his government declared independence from Great Britain.

won its independence from France in 1962, after an eight-year war. Belgium withdrew from the Congo in 1960.

British colonies became independent one after another. Among them were Ghana (1957), Nigeria (1960), Tanzania (1961), Sierra Leone and Uganda (1962), Kenya (1963), Malawi and Zambia (1964), and Botswana (1966).

Most of the newly independent African nations soon became one-party states, either by decree, rigged elections, or military coups. For example, when Malawi gained independence in 1964, the respected Dr. Hastings Banda became its first African head of state. Like a host of other African presidents, he quickly moved to acquire unbridled power and personal wealth. He established a police state and crushed revolts in 1965 and 1967. In 1970 he appointed himself president-for-life. Aided by secret police and a youth militia, Banda imprisoned and killed his opponents and looted the nation's economy. In 1994, suffering from ill health, he was forced to permit democratic elections and was defeated.

The United Nations (the UN, an international peacekeeping organization) imposed sanctions forbidding trade with Rhodesia. Only South Africa, with its white supremacist system of apartheid, and Portugal, which still ruled Rhodesia's neighbors Mozambique and Angola, offered support to Rhodesia.

Inside Rhodesia rebellion against the white power grab was inevitable. A few months after Smith's election, four black Africans set up a roadblock and killed a white man. The rebels had planned to commit a series of fire bombings but were quickly apprehended. Many white Rhodesians didn't comprehend this reaction. They genuinely believed that Africans were grateful to white people for lifting them out of their "savage" condition. Therefore, when anti-colonial combatants first clashed with Rhodesian government forces in 1966 at the Battle of Chinhoyi, many whites did not understand how such a thing could happen. Some blamed foreign Communist agitators for stirring up the sentiments of their peaceable, submissive servants. Meanwhile, Smith's government banned African nationalist organizations and either arrested or exiled their leaders.

Armed conflict continued. African nationalist troops did not fare well in conventional battles, so by 1971 they abandoned conventional warfare for the less predictable style of guerrilla warfare. Harassed by the government, black nationalist leaders went into exile in 1972 and established guerrilla bases in adjacent countries. From these bases, guerrillas intensified their attacks to overthrow Smith's government. Two black nationalist parties organized armies to fight the white supremacist government: the Zimbabwe African People's Union (ZAPU), led by Joshua Nkomo; and the Zimbabwe African National Union (ZANU), led by Robert Mugabe. The two groups operated from bases in neighboring Zambia and

JOSHUA NKOMO *(LEFT)* **WAS THE LEADER OF ZAPU. ROBERT MUGABE** *(right)* **led ZANU. Both groups worked against Zimbabwe's white supremacist government by means of guerrilla warfare.**

Mozambique. The formation of these two parties continued the long-standing competition between the Ndebele and the Shona. (Robert Mugabe is Shona, and his rival, Joshua Nkomo, was Ndebele. The Shona lived mostly in the territories of Mashonaland, and the Ndebele lived in Matabeleland.)

The world at large sympathized with the guerrillas and despised Smith and his racist regime. In response to the UN's trade sanctions, Rhodesians worked to diversify (give variety to) their largely agricultural economy. They developed industry in order to provide goods that could no longer be imported. Even though Rhodesia's economy faltered after years of warfare, the nation's minority rulers remained determined to hold out in spite of the hardships imposed by the sanctions and negative world opinion.

NAMING ZIMBABWE

Throughout its history, Zimbabwe has had a number of different names, given by the various parties that controlled it.

- Southern Rhodesia, 1895–1965—named for Cecil Rhodes
- Part of the Federation of Rhodesia and Nyasaland (Southern Rhodesia, Northern Rhodesia [present-day Zambia], and Nyasaland [present-day Malawi]), 1953–1963
- Rhodesia, 1965–1979
- Zimbabwe-Rhodesia, 1979–1980
- Zimbabwe, 1980–present. *Zimbabwe* is a word derived from one of the Bantu languages meaning "stone dwelling." The name refers to a stone fortress called the Great Zimbabwe, which dates back more than one thousand years and is located in the southern part of the nation. The Great Zimbabwe was used from about A.D. 1200 to 1450 and was first visited by the Portuguese during the 1500s. European explorers rediscovered the site by 1868. Europeans believed that Africans were an inferior race, and thus incapable of building such a complex structure, so they looked in vain for evidence of an ancient white race of Phoenicians, Arabs, or Hebrews. The site includes a hilltop fort with many rooms and passages, outer walls, a tower, several outbuildings, and an extensive drainage system. The stone structures were built without mortar and remain standing to this day. An archaeologist confirmed in 1932 that Africans built the Great Zimbabwe, but white Rhodesians continued their efforts to discredit the evidence.

For a total of eight years, the Smith government pressed the war with increasing ruthlessness, but the effort proved futile. The pressures of international economic sanctions were too great, and eventually Smith's supporters deserted him. Feeling betrayed and abandoned, Smith had to bow to the inevitable. British authorities presided over a 1979 agreement that provided for black majority rule of an independent nation to be called Zimbabwe. Then Great Britain supervised the election of a new parliamentary government. According to terms of the agreement, the guerrillas were supposed to remain peacefully in camps while the election took place.

In 1980 Nkomo's ZAPU party and Mugabe's ZANU party competed in the election for parliamentary seats. Ignoring the agreement to remain in camp, Mugabe's guerrillas intimidated voters at the polls by making sure they voted for ZANU. But few of the official observers chose to report or act on this abuse. It was a heady time for black Rhodesians and their white supporters. A new era of self-government was about to begin, and the future seemed bright.

ROBERT GABRIEL MUGABE WAS BORN ON FEBRUARY 21, 1924, a year after Rhodesia officially became a self-governing British colony. Mugabe and his family lived at Kutama, a Jesuit mission in the bush (wilderness; countryside) some 50 miles (80 km) from the capital at Salisbury. The Christian mission consisted of a few mud huts, a church, and a primary school. Robert's devoutly religious mother hoped her studious son, the third of six children, would become a priest. His father, Gabriel, who worked as the mission's carpenter, quarreled with the Jesuit priest who ran the mission, and the family was forced to leave. They moved to a village a few miles away, but the children continued to attend the mission school.

Over the next several years, Robert's two older brothers each died suddenly. It was a tragedy that afflicted many poor blacks—death from illnesses that would have been minor if good medical

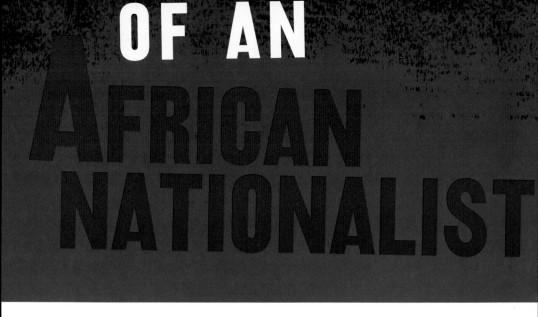

OF AN
AFRICAN
NATIONALIST

care had been available to blacks. Advanced medicine was widely available in Europe and among more affluent African whites but was not available to poor blacks. Unhinged by grief, Robert's father left the family.

By the age of ten, Robert was the oldest surviving son in his family. A new Jesuit priest, Father Jerome O'Hea, took over the mission, invited the Mugabe family to return, and encouraged Robert in his studies. Having lost his brothers, Robert grew to prefer the company of books to that of people and became the star pupil at the school. He also grew to be a devout Catholic. Father O'Hea arranged a scholarship for Robert to train as a teacher. After the training, Robert returned at the age of seventeen to teach at the mission school. He supported his mother and three younger siblings with his small salary, equivalent to just a few dollars a month.

THE YOUNG TEACHER

Just three years later, in 1944, Robert's ailing father came home to die, bringing with him three young children he had with another woman. By age twenty, Robert was supporting six younger siblings on his small salary and rising before dawn to read and study. By 1945 Robert had left the mission to teach at another mission school. He moved from school to school, never putting down roots or making friends.

Few colleges in Africa accepted black students at the time, but in 1949 Mugabe received a scholarship to attend Fort Hare University in the Eastern Cape Province of South Africa. After graduation, he resumed teaching, eventually taking a position at a teacher training college in Ghana, West Africa. There he broke out of his solitude to court Sally Hayfron, a vivacious Ghanian teacher in training. Living in Ghana was also his first experience in an independent black-governed nation. His political awareness of the inequities of Rhodesia's white supremacist government grew while he was there. In 1960 he returned to Rhodesia and gave up teaching to dedicate himself to black nationalist politics. He threw himself into working for the National Democratic Party (NDP), led by Joshua Nkomo. Sally joined Mugabe in Rhodesia, converted to Catholicism, and the two married in 1961.

Two years later, Mugabe's involvement in politics placed him in jeopardy of arrest, and he and Sally fled the country on foot. Although Sally was pregnant, the pair endured a three-day trek and had to wade across a river into neighboring Botswana to the west. They eventually reached Tanzania, where their son,

ROBERT MUGABE MARRIED SALLY HAYFRON IN 1961 AFTER MEETING HER in her home country of Ghana. She is pictured here with her husband at a 1990 independence celebration in Harare, Zimbabwe.

Nhamodzenyika (meaning "my country is in trouble"), was born. Three months after the birth, Mugabe returned to Rhodesia as a high-ranking officer—secretary general—of the newly formed black nationalist party Zimbabwe African National Union (ZANU). The black nationalist movement in Rhodesia had split into two factions based on tribal lines. Nkomo led the Ndebele-dominated Zimbabwe African People's Union (ZAPU), while Mugabe, a Shona, joined the Shona-oriented ZANU.

A GENEALOGY OF POLITICAL PARTIES

Rhodesia's branch of the African National Congress (ANC)—a political organization working for majority black rule—was founded in 1957 by Joshua Nkomo and was banned by the government in 1959. The party reorganized as the National Democratic Party (NDP) in 1960 and was banned in 1961. That same year, ZAPU formed in its place but was banned in 1962.

In Tanzania ZANU, led by Ndabaningi Sithole, split off from ZAPU in 1963. The Zimbabwe African National Liberation Army (ZANLA), the military wing of ZANU, formed in 1964. The Rhodesian government banned ZANU the same year. The Zimbabwe People's Revolutionary Army (ZIPRA), the military wing of ZAPU, formed in 1965.

THE POLITICAL PRISONER

By this time, Rhodesia's black townships had been rocked by unrest, and the white government began jailing black leaders under the repressive Law and Order Maintenance Act. Robert Mugabe had reentered Rhodesia knowing that he, too, as a prominent nationalist leader, would be jailed. In December 1963, without formal charges or a trial, and on the basis of the assumption that he was "likely to commit acts of violence," Mugabe was sent to prison. He remained a political prisoner for nearly eleven years. During that time, Prime Minister Ian Smith declared Rhodesia an independent white-ruled nation. Also during that time, Mugabe's son, whom he had not seen since infancy, died of malaria in Ghana. (Sally and Nhamodzenyika had not accompanied Mugabe back to Rhodesia. As a political activist in her own right, Sally also would have faced arrest. Instead, she returned with her son to Ghana, her homeland.) Although prison officials were willing to let Mugabe attend his son's funeral, Smith personally forbade it.

With much of the black leadership languishing as political prisoners, the black nationalist movement in Rhodesia failed to gather strength. At this time, measures imposed by Smith's government were successfully suppressing the black nationalism movement. From behind bars, Mugabe, when not pursuing his studies, began maneuvering for control of his ZANU party and a leadership role in the coming armed rebellion. His first goal was to topple the Reverend Ndabaningi Sithole, who was also in prison, and replace him as ZANU party leader.

Mugabe used his time in prison to pursue an ever-expanding education. By correspondence course, he earned several college degrees, including education and law degrees. When prison authorities intercepted the mail containing his law books, Mugabe's wife—who had taken refuge in London—copied passages by hand and sent the pages in her letters to him.

BOTH MUGABE AND NDABANINGI SITHOLE *(ABOVE CENTER)* **WERE IN PRISON** when Mugabe replaced Sithole as head of the ZANU party in 1974. Party leaders believed Mugabe would be more likely to be successful through the use of radical tactics.

Sithole himself paved the way for his own downfall in 1969 by declaring his opposition to an armed rebellion against Rhodesia. Throughout history, during times of conflict and rebellion, leaders who advocate violent tactics often attract more support than leaders who advocate less radical tactics. So it was in 1974 when highly placed members of ZANU voted to replace Sithole with Mugabe, who supported the violent overthrow of Smith's government.

Smith's white supremacist government was isolated by the economic sanctions imposed by most of the world community. To maintain white control, Smith needed support from fellow white supremacist governments in neighboring Mozambique and South Africa. However, black nationalist guerrillas began achieving notable victories against Mozambique's white-controlled government. In response Portugal, which had been the European power controlling Mozambique, abruptly abandoned its colony to the nationalists.

Next, South Africa's white minority government bowed to pressure from black nationalist governments in the region and pressured Smith to release his political prisoners and declare a cease-fire. Smith did so, releasing the leadership of ZANU and ZAPU, including Nkomo, Sithole, and Mugabe, all of whom left Salisbury Prison in December 1974. After a brief stay at his sister's house, Mugabe fled Rhodesia in April, arriving on foot in Mozambique to assume command of his party's guerrilla army there. Soon the cease-fire broke down and fighting resumed between Rhodesian government forces and the rebels.

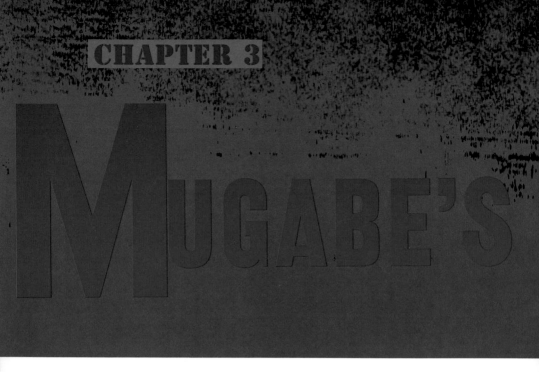

CHAPTER 3

MUGABE'S

THE FIGHT BY BLACK NATIONALIST GUERRILLAS to overthrow Smith's government intensified during the 1970s. Two guerrilla forces joined together to participate in the war they called the Second Chimurenga. The military wing of ZAPU, called the Zimbabwe People's Revolutionary Army (ZIPRA), was led by Joshua Nkomo, a longtime nationalist. Based in Zambia, ZIPRA received support from the Soviet Union (present-day Russia and its fifteen surrounding republics). ZANU's military arm, the Zimbabwe African National Liberation Army (ZANLA), was based in Mozambique and received support from the People's Republic of China. Thus China and the Soviet Union, the world's two most powerful Communist rival nations, were supporting opposing black nationalist movements in their effort to overthrow Rhodesia's government.

Robert Mugabe had been named the head of ZANU in 1974. But

his assumption of leadership over the guerrillas in Mozambique was delayed first by his imprisonment, then by his escape from Rhodesia, and finally by conflict within the party. Mugabe achieved dominance over ZANLA in mid-1976. Under his command, thousands of guerrillas reentered Rhodesia and began attacking white-owned farms. Josiah Tongogara organized the attacks, while Mugabe broadcast inflammatory, hate-filled speeches to rally support for his cause.

A GENERATION AT WAR

The war consumed a generation of young Rhodesians. Young whites died with the belief that they were defending their homes and way

YOUNG GUERRILLAS FROM MUGABE'S ZANLA STAGE A RALLY IN EARLY 1980. Many young blacks joined the fight for majority black rule.

of life. Young blacks died with the belief that they were fighting to regain their ancestral homeland. Atrocities were committed on both sides. On two occasions, the rebels shot down a civilian airliner, while the Rhodesian air force bombed several refugee camps. Both sides tortured and killed civilians in an effort to extract information about the enemy. An estimated 30,000 people died during the Second Chimurenga.

Black African villagers of the rural borderlands suffered at the hands of both armies. Supporters of Rhodesia's armed forces called the African nationalist guerrillas "terrorists," but government soldiers used terror to try to win the war. Rhodesian soldiers tortured and killed villagers in an attempt to get information about the guerrillas' whereabouts. Rhodesians also forced tens of thousands of villagers into internment camps to "protect" them from the nationalists, but it was really to prevent them from assisting and feeding the guerrillas. They burned entire villages and fields full of crops to prevent the villagers from trying to return to their homes, and they poisoned water sources to prevent guerrillas from using them.

Most African villagers of Rhodesia aided the guerrillas—whom they called freedom fighters—whenever possible, carrying messages and providing food and clothing. However, the guerrillas also terrorized the villagers, accusing some of spying for the enemy. They made examples of suspects by torturing and killing them in front of their families.

THESE WOMEN HAVE BEEN PLACED IN AN INTERNMENT CAMP, CALLED A protected village by Rhodesian officials. These villages were set up in the 1970s to prevent people from giving aid to the nationalist guerrillas.

Rhodesia's white farmers bore the brunt of guerrilla raids, and many lost their lives to ambushes, gunfire, and land mines. Some fled to Rhodesia's cities or to South Africa. Those who stayed on their farms mounted patrols and traveled in convoys to increase safety.

THE BEGINNING OF THE END

In 1976 Mugabe and Nkomo formed a unified party, the Patriotic Front. Great Britain, the United States, and the African states belonging to the Organization of African Unity

WHITE RHODESIAN COMMANDOS prepare to fight back against black nationalist guerrillas along the Mozambique border.

(OAU) announced their support for the Patriotic Front. Smith, however, was unwilling to work with the two guerrilla leaders. Instead, he signed an agreement with Mugabe's old rivals, Ndabaningi Sithole and the black Methodist bishop Abel Muzorewa. The 1979 parliamentary election in Rhodesia—the first in which blacks could vote—gave the twenty-eight allocated white seats to Smith's party and a majority of the seventy-two African seats to Muzorewa's party, making Muzorewa prime minister.

However, Smith still exerted control behind the scenes. Moreover, whites still controlled the judiciary, civil service, and security forces. Whites had veto power over all legislation, and white land ownership remained untouchable. Rhodesia became known as Zimbabwe-Rhodesia. The guerrillas responded by stepping up their campaign of violence.

At the same time, African leaders such as Kenneth Kaunda of Zambia and Samora Machel of Mozambique urged Nkomo and Mugabe to negotiate an end to the war. Both nations had suffered economically from years of supporting Rhodesian guerrilla bases. From September to December 1979, Smith, Muzorewa, Nkomo, and Mugabe attended the Lancaster House Conference in London.

After tough negotiations, Smith conceded that Rhodesia would

FRONT ROW, FROM LEFT TO RIGHT: **BISHOP ABEL MUZOREWA, LORD CARRINGTON,** Sir Ian Gilmore, Joshua Nkomo, and Robert Mugabe sign the 1979 agreement for black majority rule reached during the Lancaster House Conference in London.

become Zimbabwe and be governed by the black majority. A new constitution was to allow for majority rule and protection of minority rights. Britain and the United States helped to break an impasse (deadlock) over land redistribution by promising funds for blacks to purchase white-owned land. Rhodesia briefly returned to British colony status, and a cease-fire took effect. The Patriotic Front agreed to abide by a British-prepared interim (temporary) constitution for ten years. Among its provisions was one to honor the

IN THEIR OWN WORDS

After the war for independence came to an end, black Zimbabweans expected their lives to improve, while some white Rhodesians held fast to their racist beliefs and dreaded life under black majority rule. Here is a sampling of what they had to say:

Black village teacher's wife: "We used to think that only the white man could have water in his house. . . . It was only after the war that people began to understand that they had rights. . . . People in Zimbabwe are now free. . . . "

White woman in Harare: "It was us who made this country great, not them. They were practically still living in trees when we came."

Black villager: "There is a lot of development in Zimbabwe today because we are now doing things for ourselves. We even built the school for ourselves. Although the government helped us, this is true development. Now we can say that Zimbabwe is free. . . . [W]ith the school, we decided that we would make the bricks and build it and we did just that."

Former prime minister of Rhodesia, Ian Smith, on his refusal to

property rights of white landowners. The black nationalists had hoped to redistribute white-owned farmland as soon as they gained independence. But according to the terms of the Lancaster House Agreement, they had to put this off for ten years. In addition, the Patriotic Front leadership appeared to understand that they could not afford to drive off the white population because the whites possessed unique skills, particularly in the agricultural sector, as well as capital to fund economic growth.

attend Mugabe's inauguration: "The thought of being confronted by a scene where [the British] would be wringing their hands in apparent pleasure, and fawning around a bunch of communist terrorists who had come into their position through intimidation, corruption, and a blatantly dishonest election, was a situation against which my whole system would revolt. . . . Then to add insult to injury, they planned to compound the felony by using the Queen's young son to crown the glorious proceedings by pulling down the Union Jack [British flag], thence to be consigned to the rubbish heap."

Joannah Nkomo, wife of defeated ZAPU candidate Joshua Nkomo: "When we heard that ZANU had won and would rule the country, we were disappointed: although I was also very relieved that those who had won were blacks. . . . Independence Day was a great day. . . . We were treated well and taken to places we had never been to before, places that had been prohibited . . . and it was a great moment to see black people in high places ruling. . . . It was also good to meet Robert Mugabe and his wife. . . . We all met as one people and that was wonderful."

The war to establish black rule in Rhodesia presented the Western world with a dilemma. While most Western nations abhorred Ian Smith's racist regime, they feared that a black victory—aided by China and the Soviet Union—would aid the expansion of Communism. Communism is a political, social, and economic model based on the idea that property should be state-owned rather than private. The Communist model also says that all citizens should have equal resources and be of equal social status. (Capitalism, in contrast, is based on ideas of economic freedom and individual property.) Mugabe made no secret of his admiration for Communist dictators such as Joseph Stalin of the Soviet Union and Fidel Castro of Cuba. Mugabe openly talked about his plans to establish a Communist regime in Rhodesia. This appealed to many blacks, who hoped Communism would provide equitable sharing of resources. The white supremacist rulers of Rhodesia had implemented a capitalist system, but one that denied black people the educational and economic resources that promote success under capitalism. As a result, many black Rhodesians saw Communism as the way to redress generations of inequality.

THE FIRST ELECTION

British-supervised parliamentary elections were planned. However, white Rhodesians feared for the future, seeing the two major candidates, Robert Mugabe and Joshua Nkomo, as Communist warlords. Mugabe's wartime pronouncements, such as "Let us rid our home of this settler vermin," had convinced them that they would no longer be safe. Rival candidate Nkomo had only

A WOMAN CASTS HER VOTE IN THE 1980 PARLIAMENTARY ELECTION, THE first election in a free Zimbabwe. The sample ballot behind her is written in Shona, a local language.

a slightly more moderate reputation. However, neither white Rhodesians nor the world community understood the extent of the rivalry between the two black leaders.

Nkomo had been a leader of the black nationalist movement since the 1950s and had spent ten years as a political prisoner. He had hoped that the two parties would remain united under the Patriotic Front for the upcoming election. However, Mugabe insisted on running a separate campaign for ZANU. He was confident that his Shona supporters would triumph over Nkomo's party, ZAPU, which was the party of the minority Ndebele people. Eighty seats in Parliament were contested by black candidates. Twenty seats were reserved for whites. The voting took place over the last three days of February 1980. The result was announced on March 3, giving Mugabe's party, ZANU, a majority in Parliament. ZANU won fifty-six seats, while Nkomo's ZAPU won twenty. This victory allowed Mugabe to take the position of prime minister.

According to the memoirs of both Ian Smith and Joshua Nkomo, Mugabe's party had intimidated voters into supporting him, using tactics such as murdering opposition campaign workers and beating up opposition supporters. Both recalled that the British election observers were aware of the violence but chose not to challenge the election results because they were unwilling to delay Zimbabwe's long-awaited independence. It is notable that Mugabe almost certainly would have won the election because his Shona supporters outnumbered the opposition. Nonetheless, he chose violence to ensure his own election.

After the elections, black Zimbabweans danced in the streets. Many white Rhodesians—fearful of black majority rule—began putting their homes up for sale, closing their businesses, removing their children from the soon-to-be integrated schools, and heading for South Africa, where white supremacist rule still existed.

In Zimbabwe's capital city of Salisbury, soon to be renamed Harare, Robert Gabriel Mugabe took the oath of office just before midnight on April 17, 1980, promising to faithfully serve Zimbabwe as prime minister. The flag of Rhodesia came down at midnight and was replaced by the flag of independent Zimbabwe. In attendance at the packed soccer stadium were Great Britain's Prince Charles, Lord Soames (the last British governor of Rhodesia), and an honor guard composed of soldiers from three armies. Troops from the two black guerrilla forces and the white security force of Rhodesia marched together.

SUPPORTERS CELEBRATE MUGABE'S INAUGURATION AS PRIME MINISTER OF
Zimbabwe in April 1980, after years under white supremacist rule.

The first broadcast words of the new prime minister—whose threatening and hate-filled wartime speeches had sown such terror—astounded Smith, the white population, and observers around the world. Mugabe said: "I urge you, whether you are black or white, to join me in a new pledge to forget our grim past . . . join hands in a new amity and together, as Zimbabweans, trample upon racism." Mugabe seemed to stay true to his promise when he invited white officials to stay in their government and army jobs and when he appointed Joshua Nkomo and other

A GOVERNMENT
OF RECONCILIATION

In 1980 newly elected Robert Mugabe invited chief rival Joshua Nkomo to accept the nation's ceremonial office of president. Nkomo refused the offer but agreed to serve as minister of Home Affairs, which put him in charge of the police force.

With twenty of one hundred seats in Parliament reserved for whites, two former Rhodesian prime ministers, Ian Smith and Garfield Todd, became members of Parliament. Other white people were offered government positions as well. Most notably, David Smith, former deputy prime minister to Ian Smith, became minister of Trade and Commerce; Ken Flower remained as chief of the Central Intelligence Organization; and Denis Norman, a leading commercial farmer, became minister of Agriculture. Mugabe also invited General Peter Walls, the commander of the Rhodesian army, to stay on as commander of the new Zimbabwean army, a unified force of some eighty thousand men drawn from ZANLA, ZIPRA, and the Rhodesian army.

members of the rival ZAPU to his cabinet. He assured white farmers and business owners that they had a secure future in Zimbabwe. He also promised that the change from capitalism to Communism would be gradual. With these actions, Mugabe successfully reversed the tide of white flight.

Mugabe's conciliatory words and actions brought him international goodwill, favorable publicity, and pledges of generous foreign aid. It remained to be seen whether he could or would fulfill his promises to the new nation.

A Zimbabwean human rights lawyer later commented, "The world looked the other way when Mugabe took over in 1980. . . . Mugabe had risen to power in the nationalist movement by collaborating in the murder and intimidation of anyone who stood in his way. . . . [I]t was clear to anyone who cared to scan the evidence that the man was a thug."

ZIMBABWE APPEARED TO BLOSSOM after the war and the attainment of independence. Black Zimbabweans reveled in their right to full participation in society. Funded by foreign aid, Robert Mugabe announced government programs to expand education and health care. During the first two years of Mugabe's regime, plentiful rains brought abundant harvests. And Mugabe's conciliatory policy toward the white population set the stage for substantial economic growth.

1980–1981: THE OPENING MOVES

In his first months in office, Mugabe had several cordial meetings with his former enemy, Ian Smith. Smith remained active in

DATELINE TO DESPOTISM

government, serving as the opposition leader in the Zimbabwean Parliament. He recalled that Mugabe appeared to be fair-minded and reasonable at their meetings. However, the Zimbabwean media soon began broadcasting inflammatory antiwhite and pro-Communist statements by cabinet ministers. Mugabe told Smith that he was unaware of these broadcasts, but Smith began to doubt him.

In spite of the promising dawn of peace, the bitterness of the war years lingered for black and white veterans alike. White veterans lived with the sting of having lost a long and brutal war and feared they had no future in Zimbabwe. African veterans faced a different challenge. Many of them had left home as children to join the freedom fighters. They confronted the future with no formal education or job skills with which to join the nation's peacetime economy.

ZIMBABWE: THE LAND

Zimbabwe is a highland country with only a few places that are lower than 1,000 feet (304 meters) above sea level. The nation's major geographical feature is a broad central ridge about 50 miles (80 km) wide that extends for 400 miles (643 km) across the entire country. Most of this ridge is between 4,000 and 5,000 feet (1,219 and 1,524 m) high. This ridge covers about one-quarter of Zimbabwe's land area and is called the Highveld. The pleasant climate of the Highveld attracted European settlers. The word *veld* comes from the Dutch language and means "grassland."

The land slopes away from this central ridge to form a wide upland, or plateau region, with an altitude of between 3,000 and 4,000 feet (914 and 1,219 m). This region is called the Middleveld and makes up some 40 percent of Zimbabwe's land area. Several large rivers flow through southern Zimbabwe. These river valleys, called the Lowveld, form the rest of Zimbabwe.

Zimbabwe is located along a tropical latitude, but because the land is so elevated, temperatures are cooler. Although there are some arid areas in the Lowveld, much of Zimbabwe receives a generous amount of seasonal rain brought by monsoons from the Indian Ocean. Consequently, the land is largely savanna (or veld), with lush grassland and many trees. The northeastern part of the country receives more than twice as much annual rainfall as the southwestern region. Much of the rain falls in heavy showers during a few months of the rainy season. Hot, dry weather follows. This seasonal pattern makes growing crops difficult. Poor soil also hampers agriculture. Conflict over who should own and farm the best land has played an important role in Zimbabwe's history.

The only skills they possessed were military skills, and the new Zimbabwean army and police force could not absorb all of them.

After the war, the fighting men of ZANLA and ZIPRA had been ordered into camps called "assembly points" to await demobilization and reintegration into society. Unemployment quickly became a problem, as Mugabe's ruling ZANU party gave most of the available jobs and land to the former ZANLA men. Some disaffected former ZIPRA men lost patience, deserted, and turned to crime. Inflammatory speeches by Mugabe's leading ZANU officials encouraged ex-ZANLA soldiers to harass members of the rival party. Inevitably, armed skirmishes broke out between ex-soldiers of the two parties.

GUERRILLAS OF ZIPRA MEET AT AN ASSEMBLY POINT IN ZIMBABWE IN January 1980 to be demobilized. Many of these men turned to crime when promises of land did not materialize.

Abandoning his stated intention to include members of all parties in Zimbabwe's government, Mugabe seized upon the unrest as an excuse to persecute the principal rival party. He had nine important ZAPU officials arrested and held without trial. When Joshua Nkomo, minister of Home Affairs with oversight of the police, refused to sign the detention orders, somebody stole his official seal and used it to forge the documents. In January 1981, Mugabe removed Nkomo from his important cabinet post and reassigned him to a trivial one. The following month, more fighting occurred between the two former guerrilla armies, resulting in more than 300 deaths.

By March 1981, just a year after his election, Mugabe announced his intention to make Zimbabwe a one-party Communist state. By July he was publicly calling for violence against whites who did not support him. At the time, Zimbabwe had fewer than 6,000 white commercial farmers. Yet they played a vital economic role. They grew 90 percent of the country's staple crop, maize, and produced 90 percent of the main commercial crop, cotton. Their export crops accounted for one-third of the nation's total exports. Most important, they employed about one-third of the wage-earning labor force. Mugabe's threats frightened whites, who began leaving the country in large numbers.

Under Mugabe's direction, the country slid into lawlessness. Mugabe declared himself above the law by stating that he could ignore any court decisions with which he disagreed. Ian Smith and others who belonged to opposition parties, whether white or black, were harassed, arrested, searched, and interrogated. The government nationalized (took control of) a number of businesses. (Nationalizing businesses can be a popular symbolic action for a government, especially if the public believes that the business owners are wealthy and obtained that wealth unfairly.)

Zimbabwean business owners feared that if they opposed the regime, their businesses would be targeted for nationalization.

By the terms of an agreement worked out when Zimbabwe became independent, the guerrilla armies were supposed to disband. Accordingly, in May 1981, Nkomo ordered his ZIPRA army to disband. Around the same time, much of Mugabe's ZANU army also disbanded. However, the previous year Mugabe had decided to keep an army brigade to deal with his political opponents. He signed a secret agreement with North Korea, a brutal Communist dictatorship, to train this brigade. This force became the infamous Fifth Brigade, answerable only to ZANU-loyalist officers appointed by Mugabe. Its soldiers were all from Mugabe's Shona tribe. Its role was strictly to suppress political opposition among Zimbabwean citizens.

Mugabe did not conceal his intentions. In fact, he allowed his subordinates to issue public warnings. Edgar Tekere, one of his strongmen, said, "Nkomo and his guerrillas are germs in the country's wounds, and they will have to be cleaned up with iodine. The patient will have to scream a bit."

1982–1984:
BEHEADING THE COBRA

In February 1982, police raided two farms owned by members of ZAPU and discovered arms stockpiles there. Though the stockpiles may have dated back to the war, Mugabe seized on their presence as a reason to accuse Nkomo of plotting to overthrow the government. He ousted Nkomo and other ZAPU-loyal cabinet ministers from the government.

Seven prominent former ZIPRA officers were arrested and charged with treason. In April 1983, Zimbabwe's High Court cleared them. They were rearrested at the courthouse and held indefinitely without charge. After Nkomo's dismissal, Mugabe said, "ZAPU and its leader, Dr. Joshua Nkomo, are like a cobra in the house. The only way to deal effectively with a snake is to strike and destroy its head." Over the next months, more than a dozen prominent ZAPU members were killed by men in uniform. Members of the Fifth Brigade raided Nkomo's home in Bulawayo and murdered three of his employees. The Fifth Brigade cordoned off areas of the city to search for Nkomo, but he escaped to Botswana.

Mugabe announced that the nation had a dissident problem and declared a state of emergency (a common tool of dictators). He moved to neutralize the ZAPU threat by sending the Fifth Brigade into Matabeleland, the homeland of the Ndebele, many of whom were ZAPU supporters. Again he did not conceal his intentions: "We have to deal with this problem quite ruthlessly." Beginning in January 1983, the Fifth Brigade began operations, using tactics developed during the fight for independence and refined through training with the North Koreans. Soldiers would suddenly enter a village and round up everyone. They would order villagers to sing songs praising Mugabe and his party. They would then select a few villagers for beatings and torture in order to intimidate the others. The soldiers also used torture to extract confessions of disloyalty. Having identified the "dissidents," they then executed them. The purpose was to terrorize the survivors into supporting Mugabe's government.

A group of Catholic bishops in Matabeleland issued a statement in the spring of 1983 based on their observations in the area:

"The facts point to a reign of terror caused by wanton [unrestrained] killings, woundings, beatings, burnings, and rapings. Many homes have been burnt down. People in rural areas are starving, not only because of the drought, but because in some cases supplies of food have been deliberately cut off and in other cases access to food supplies has been restricted or stopped. The innocent have no recourse or redress, for fear of reprisals." Since then little information about the atrocities of the Fifth Brigade has come to light, although mass graves have been discovered in the region. Estimates of the death toll range from 10,000 to 40,000 people.

In 1984 the Fifth Brigade expanded its terror campaign farther into Matabeleland, blocking all food deliveries and closing stores. A Fifth Brigade officer told the starving inhabitants, "First you will eat your chickens, then your goats, then your cattle, then your donkeys. Then you will eat your children and finally you will eat the dissidents."

Mugabe's secret police joined with the Fifth Brigade to extend the reign of terror. While the Fifth Brigade systematically starved the people of Matabeleland, the secret police rounded up thousands of civilians on the slightest suspicion of being ZAPU supporters and herded them into army camps. Here they tortured them to death, dumping their bodies in abandoned mine shafts where they could never be counted or identified. Mugabe publicly praised his

MUGABE'S ENFORCERS

In the twenty-first century, Zimbabwe has two police forces. The Zimbabwe Republic Police is the regular national police force. Although it is supposed to provide law enforcement for the nation regardless of who holds political power, it has increasingly acted to carry out the dictates of Mugabe and the ruling party. The other force, known as the secret police, consists of operatives for Zimbabwe's Central Intelligence Organization, who act covertly, seeking out and arresting anyone deemed to be an enemy of the Mugabe regime.

When Mugabe rose to power in 1980, he also created two organizations answerable only to his ruling political party: the Fifth Brigade and the Youth League. The Youth League, in turn, formed youth brigades. The Fifth Brigade and the Youth League employ violence to terrorize Zimbabweans security forces for performing their duty well. He called the police war against his people *gukurahundi,* a Shona word that means "storm that blows away chaff." His intent was to rid the nation of all opposition to his rule.

1985–1987: A LAW UNTO HIMSELF

In 1985 national elections were held. Mugabe issued further threats against his political rivals, primarily supporters of Nkomo's ZAPU party. He unleashed politically indoctrinated youth brigades to intimidate voters in Matabeleland. These brigades acted like lawless gangs, forcing people to join Mugabe's ZANU party and beating those who resisted. Prominent ZAPU politicians disappeared during the night, never to be seen again.

In spite of the violence, ZAPU won all the parliamentary seats in Matabeleland. This enraged Mugabe. Overall, though, Mugabe's ZANU party elected a solid majority to Parliament, making Mugabe prime minister for another term. After a victory tainted by violence, Mugabe's supporters rampaged through the streets and wrecked the homes of opposition candidates.

Mugabe then turned his attention to destroying ZAPU. He appointed a brutal new police minister. One week after the elections, the police again raided Nkomo's home and arrested his aides. Further raids collected several hundred ZAPU officials. The police minister announced, "We want to wipe out the ZAPU leadership." Step by step, government security forces dismantled the

ZAPU party by banning its rallies and meetings and dissolving regional associations controlled by ZAPU.

1987–1990: "UNITY"

After years of terror in Matabeleland, Mugabe enticed the few surviving "dissidents" into joining a new Unity Party, offering them amnesty (pardon). He opened discussions with the surviving ZAPU members and assured Nkomo of his safety.

A major reason Mugabe ended the terror campaign against Matabeleland was related to developments outside of Zimbabwe. At the time, the white supremacist government in South Africa was sponsoring a rebel faction in neighboring Mozambique. These rebels threatened to cut Zimbabwe's railroad connection with Beira, Mozambique, a port on the Indian Ocean. Beira was important because it was the port through which most of Zimbabwe's imports and exports flowed. Back in 1986, Mugabe had sent Zimbabwean military forces into Mozambique to secure the railway. By 1988 the fighting had intensified and spread. So Mugabe shifted military resources from his campaign against the Ndebele of Matabeleland to the conflict in Mozambique. The Zimbabwean military successfully secured the transportation corridor to Beira in 1989. With this success, Mugabe decided that he was done with foreign wars.

On December 22, 1987, Nkomo and Mugabe signed a Unity Accord that brought Nkomo and a few other ZAPU leaders back into the cabinet. The two parties merged under the name of ZANU-Patriotic Front (ZANU-PF), and ZAPU was dissolved. Nkomo never spoke publicly about his reasons for signing ZAPU out of

on the Indian Ocean. The port is critical to land-locked nations such as Zimbabwe, which have no natural access to the sea.

existence. Near the end of his life, he told an interviewer that, by doing so, he had hoped to end the violence against his people.

Three days after the signing of the Unity Accord, Robert Mugabe was inaugurated as president amid great pomp and ceremony. Earlier in 1987, he had pushed through changes to the Zimbabwean constitution that made him president, with the right to run for reelection an unlimited number of times. Mugabe had also tightened the screws against the white minority by abolishing the seats in Parliament that were reserved for them. Because of these changes, after December 1987 Mugabe held absolute power to control everyone and everything in Zimbabwe.

Mugabe had always made clear his desire for one-party Communist-style rule, with himself as the unchallenged head of that one party. Ian Smith, who resigned from Parliament at this time and is a highly biased source, related a conversation with a high-ranking minister of the era that has the ring of truth. This minister explained the Mugabe government's reason for adopting

Communist principles: "It has nothing to do with the philosophy of communism, which is foreign to us. . . . What appealed to us most . . . was the firm instruction that: 'Once you become the government, you remain the government forever.'"

To hold on to power, Mugabe developed a comprehensive patronage system. This meant that he rewarded his loyalists by appointing them to positions in the government and media or giving them jobs paid by the state. The opportunity to have a paying job was the "carrot," or the lure. The "stick," or threat, was always the fear of what would happen if a loyalist became an opponent.

Meanwhile, Zimbabwe's government grew ever more expensive to run, with too many officials spending public money to indulge in luxuries such as travel to numerous foreign conferences. The money they spent would have funded much of the nation's education and health care systems. Public officials also took over farms that white people had abandoned, thus denying them to the general population. Excessive government spending caused runaway inflation, and government price controls limiting what farmers could charge for food crops caused agricultural production to plummet to half of what it had been in the early 1980s.

Students at Zimbabwe's university in Harare protested government corruption. So in 1989, Mugabe closed down the university and ordered the arrest of students and professors. As the economy continued to flounder, political opposition within Zimbabwe to the Mugabe regime began to solidify among the dispossessed and disappointed. For example, the Zimbabwe Congress of Trade Unions, led by Morgan Tsvangirai, objected to the university closing. So Tsvangirai was arrested.

A rival emerged from within Mugabe's own political party. His name was Edgar Tekere. In the past, Tekere had been one of

EDGAR TEKERE GIVES A PRESS CONFERENCE IN ANGOLA IN JANUARY 1990.
His party, the Zimbabwe Unity Movement (ZUM), challenged Mugabe's ZANU-PF in the 1990 Zimbabwe election.

Mugabe's strongmen, issuing threats and cracking down on opponents. He had also used his position for personal gain. However, during the time before the scheduled 1990 election, Tekere reinvented himself as a leader who was against corruption.

Since Nkomo and Mugabe had merged their parties as ZANU-PF, Mugabe faced opposition in the 1990 elections only from Tekere's Zimbabwe Unity Movement (ZUM). Mugabe considered ZUM a serious threat to his control over the country. A few days before the election, an important ZUM political leader was shot by one of Mugabe's loyalists. The day before the election, five ZUM candidates withdrew, fearing for their safety. Overall, threats, attacks, and a variety of official obstacles raised by Mugabe's regime reduced the number of opposition candidates. Consequently, in an unfree election, Tekere's party won only two seats in Parliament. Moreover, the nation's judiciary was now largely dominated by people who answered only to Mugabe. When a judge sentenced several men to prison because of their involvement in attacks against Mugabe's political foes, Mugabe overrode the judge and pardoned them. Another ten years would pass before a new and effective political challenge to Mugabe's rule would emerge.

1991–1999: ABSOLUTE POWER

The 1990s saw Zimbabwe decline by every measure. For example, by 1993 the rate of inflation was 50 percent, while interest on loans was a staggering 55 percent. For average citizens, this meant they could barely afford everyday necessities. What little money they possessed had declined in value, and they could not afford the cost of borrowing money. In a bid to distract the public from the declining economy, in December 1990 Parliament had passed a constitutional amendment giving it the authority to confiscate (seize) land at whatever price it set. This was a politically popular move since whites continued to own some of the country's best farmland. The government began taking over working white-owned farms for minimal compensation, and within a few years simply confiscated them. However, many of these productive farms were given to government officials and party supporters, who used them only as country estates. A few farms were turned over to randomly selected inexperienced black farmers, who could not maintain profitable crop yields. Thus, land redistribution resulted in a huge loss of agricultural production. Some of the first farms to be taken were owned by vocal opponents of Mugabe's rule. When whites appealed to the nation's courts for legal protection, Mugabe replied that he would do what he wanted regardless of what the courts said. Later in the decade, the government seized farms owned by blacks who opposed Mugabe. It was just one more way Mugabe operated to intimidate and silence anyone who opposed him. Furthermore, during the 1990s, another bad drought came to southern Africa.

In the face of devastating economic decline, Mugabe worried about how best to keep his close supporters from rebelling. His answer was to continue to spend large sums on a bloated civil service and army. He particularly needed to keep the army happy to prevent a coup (violent overthrow of a government). Under Mugabe's orders, officials stole foreign aid meant for things such as health care for the poor and spent it instead on maintaining the government and army. As the economy in Zimbabwe collapsed, the government responded to reports of doctor and medicine shortages by claiming that it lacked money. Parliament, dominated by Mugabe's party, then voted huge pay raises for Mugabe and his ministers. Mugabe's cronies took advantage of the prevailing corruption to increase their own wealth and high standard of living.

Resentment against Mugabe increased among the general population. People saw their lives either not improving or getting worse. From time to time, Zimbabweans spoke up against the government. Mugabe put down his opponents with threats and violence. At the same time, to try to dampen discontent, Mugabe fed racial hatred by blaming all the problems on whites. "It makes absolute nonsense of our history as an African country," Mugabe said, "that most of our arable and ranching land is still in the hands

In his political speeches, Robert Mugabe has painted the British as the enemy, but in his private life, he has tried to resemble an English gentleman. Mugabe has always dressed in the Western style and worn smartly tailored suits. He speaks perfect English with a British accent. Until 1999 he enjoyed visiting London, staying in luxurious hotel rooms, and shopping at Harrods, the famous London department store. Mugabe has also been a devoted fan of the British sport of cricket.

of our [former] colonisers, while the majority of our peasant community still live like squatters in their God-given land."

Mugabe's ploy worked because of Zimbabwe's history. Whites had indeed taken the best land and created a government that maintained white power at the expense of the black population. By constantly speaking about this history with passion and skill, Mugabe successfully diverted attention away from the failures and crimes of his own government. In particular, Mugabe's speeches diverted attention from the fact that he and his government had failed to implement real land reform.

Mugabe's behavior assumed a familiar pattern. Whenever a parliamentary or presidential election approached, he resorted to ever more severe measures to suppress his opponents. In 1995 his party easily dominated the parliamentary election, because the opposition was poorly organized. The following year, Mugabe enjoyed his last personal triumph when he won reelection as president. These two elections were the last full mandates (authorizations to rule) he ever received. Henceforth, opponents to his regime began to organize more effectively.

A major sign of this better organization emerged when opponents of the government created the Foundation for Democracy in Zimbabwe. Several dozen labor unions and political groups organized a National Constitutional Association in an attempt to change the constitution to limit the power of the presidency. Mugabe responded by establishing a four hundred–member commission to review the constitution. The commission did exactly what Mugabe wanted by issuing a report advocating a strong presidency.

Late in 1996, Mugabe wed a second wife, Grace Marufu, with whom he already had two children. His well-respected first wife, Sally, had died in 1992, and some observers believe that his

MUGABE AND HIS SECOND WIFE, GRACE MARUFU, MARRIED IN 1996 AT the Kutama Jesuit mission where Mugabe had attended school as a boy.

behavior as a dictator grew more extreme after her death. At a time when the great majority of people were suffering from the nation's severe economic downturn, Mugabe and Grace had a lavish wedding. Mugabe looted the nation's treasury to pay for food and entertainment for the couple's twelve thousand guests. Impoverished workers across the nation went on strike to protest their meager pay in light of this misuse of the country's money. Mugabe responded by threatening to fire them if they did not return to work.

The most serious threat to the Mugabe regime emerged from a surprising group. They were the war veterans, soldiers who had fought alongside Mugabe and ZANU to win independence. They saw government officials growing rich while they became poorer. The veterans staged a series of protests, but Mugabe refused to meet with them. His refusal caused them to become more demanding, and they threatened civil war. Mugabe finally gave in and promised the veterans new benefits, including pensions and land for resettlement. He ordered more farms taken from the whites to be given to the veterans.

Discontent also cropped up among students. Aware that the nation's shattered economy could not provide skilled jobs for university graduates, the students rioted in protest in 1998. Others rioted to protest the fast-rising cost of food and fuel. For the first time since Zimbabwe became independent, the government called for the army to quash the street protestors. The army ended the rioting, and Mugabe placed the universities under government control. To reward his loyal army, Mugabe ordered more seizures of white-owned farms.

At the same time, he decided to try again the strategy of involving the nation in a foreign war to distract attention from Zimbabwe's internal problems. In 1986 Mugabe had done this by sending his army into Mozambique. This time he sent his military to participate in a coalition of other African armies supporting Laurent Kabila, president of the Democratic Republic of Congo (DRC), who in 1998 was facing a violent rebellion. It was a huge drain on the already struggling Zimbabwean economy.

The Congo intervention backfired on Mugabe. It led to the formation in 1999 of the Movement for Democratic Change (MDC). The goal of the MDC was to challenge Mugabe's ruling party in the national elections of 2000. The leader of the MDC, Morgan Tsvangirai, was the leader of the Zimbabwe Congress of Trade Unions. Tsvangirai gathered support from human rights groups and religious organizations. Under his leadership, the MDC promoted a constitutional reform designed to prevent Mugabe from running for another term as president.

MORGAN TSVANGIRAI SHAKES HANDS WITH A POTENTIAL VOTER WHILE campaigning before the 2000 election.

2000–2005: CHALLENGE AND RETALIATION

Back in 1997, Mugabe had met a similar challenge to his power by establishing a commission to review the constitution. At that time, the commission did exactly what Mugabe wanted, and he survived the challenge. This time he had another commission draft a constitution. The new constitution did not challenge his presidential powers, but it did say that future presidents would be limited to two terms of five years each. The fact that Mugabe had already been in office for longer than ten years did not matter. By the terms of the new constitution, he could run for office and, when elected, serve another ten years. He was so confident in his powers that he decided to hold a national referendum in 2000 to let the people of Zimbabwe vote for the new constitution.

With the government controlling the media, radio, television, and newspapers, all encouraged voters to vote for the new constitution. In addition, Mugabe sent the army, police, and violent gangs to intimidate the opposition. In spite of the violence, 55 percent of the voters rejected the proposed constitution. It was a stunning setback for ZANU-PF. Leaders of the party quarreled about who was to blame, and many pointed their fingers at the seventy-six-year-old Mugabe, saying that the people no longer supported him.

Mugabe publicly blamed whites: "Preliminary figures show there were 100,000 white people voting," he said. "We have never had anything like that [such high numbers of voters] in this country." This record number of white votes changed the outcome, he concluded. Whether he actually believed that the white minority had been influential enough to affect the voting is unknown. However, ten days after the voting ended, he unleashed his gangs of young toughs against white landowners.

These gangs consisted mostly of unemployed urban youths. They invaded about seventy white-owned farms, attacked the farmers and their families, and threatened to kill them if they did not abandon their farms. Then the gangs remained on the land, earning the nickname "squatters." The High Court declared this behavior to be illegal, but the local police did nothing to stop it. Less than a month after voters had rejected his draft constitution, Mugabe introduced and successfully passed a new constitutional amendment that legalized the government's practice of seizing white-owned farms without compensation.

The following year, in 2001, Mugabe declared that people could not appeal to Zimbabwe's courts to be compensated for land seizures. Gangs again occupied an expanding number of farms by force. The men in these gangs called themselves war veterans, but in fact most of them were too young to have ever participated in the war for independence. Their leader was Chenjerai Hunzvi, who nicknamed himself "Hitler." Hunzvi was not a war veteran but a doctor who claimed to have earned a

CHENJERAI HUNZVI IS KNOWN for his inflammatory rhetoric and tendency to violence.

TOP: A WHITE FARMER SITS NEXT TO DEATH THREATS SCRAWLED ON THE floor of her home. *Bottom:* A squatter plows the field of a white commercial farmer who was forced off the land.

ROBERT MUGABE'S ZIMBABWE

degree while studying in Poland in the 1980s. He rose to become leader of the Zimbabwe National Liberation War Veterans Association. With thousands of actual war veterans whom he could order into the streets to march in protest against Mugabe, Hunzvi's influence grew.

Mugabe had gained Hunzvi's support by promising to give farms, bonuses, and pensions to the 50,000 people who claimed to be war veterans. The government had neither the money nor the land to keep this promise, but proceeded nevertheless. In June 2001, the government designated another 5,200 farms for confiscation. This left only about 300 farms under white ownership, thus gutting one of Zimbabwe's few remaining economically productive sectors. The consequences of the massive seizures were disastrous. Zimbabwe became an importer of its own staple crop, maize, which it had once exported. The international community protested Mugabe's actions. For the first time since Zimbabwe's independence, the United States passed economic sanctions against it. Meanwhile, many African nations accused Zimbabwe, through its collapsing economy, of destabilizing the entire regional economy.

Particularly hard hit in Zimbabwe were 300,000 to 400,000 black workers who had been employed by white commercial farmers. Because Mugabe believed these workers had voted against his constitutional referendum, he ordered a comprehensive campaign of violence against them. Gangs of "war veterans" took some workers away, never to be seen again. Others were beaten, their wives raped, and their homes destroyed. Thousands were taken to "re-education centers" that had been set up on abandoned farms, where they were harassed and beaten.

In 2002 Mugabe ran for reelection as president. His opponent was Morgan Tsvangirai of the MDC. To ensure his victory, Mugabe changed the nation's voting rules, limiting who could vote. In addition, it became a crime to criticize the president. Political meetings and rallies for anyone outside of Mugabe's party became illegal. The military declared that it would ignore the results of the election unless Mugabe won. Mugabe ordered gangs of youths, war veterans, and secret police to detain and beat MDC supporters. The gangs circulated throughout the country to hunt down suspected opponents of the government. They set up random roadblocks to pull people out of cars and buses. Anyone found carrying an MDC voter registration card became a victim. The regular police stood by and did nothing to protect them. The gangs sealed off entire regions where MDC supporters lived and subjected the population to beatings, murders, and rapes. Having already seized most of the nation's farms, Mugabe sent gangs to invade randomly selected white-owned businesses, mostly in Harare. They abducted business owners, demanded money, and confiscated vehicles and equipment.

International observers watched the voting in Zimbabwe, witnessed numerous unfair practices that denied opposition supporters the right to vote, and concluded that the election did not reflect the will of the people. The Commonwealth Observer Group (impartial election observers sent by the Commonwealth of Nations, an association of former British colonies) reported that they "were deeply impressed by the determination of the people of Zimbabwe to exercise their democratic rights." However, the group concluded the election "was marred by a high level of politically motivated violence and intimidation." In particular, youth militia groups organized by the government under a National Youth Training Program were "responsible for a systematic campaign of intimidation" against Mugabe's opponents. Although he lost and his supporters were harassed, Tsvangirai won an impressive 42 percent of the vote.

While celebrating his victory, Mugabe issued a public threat against the MDC: "We will make them run. If they haven't run before, we will make them run now." Then he turned against his opponents with even greater force. In 2003 the government charged MDC leaders, including Tsvangirai, with treason. The government did not have the evidence to make a case against Tsvangirai, but it took two years to drop the charge. The government offered no explanation for its actions.

Because of the corrupt nature of the election, both the United States and the European Union refused to recognize Mugabe's victory. Zimbabwe was suspended from membership in the Commonwealth of Nations. These measures did little to protect the citizens of Zimbabwe against their dictator. Under his orders, political and human rights activists were beaten, tortured, or killed. Mugabe made a final move against the remaining white farmers. He ordered them to leave their land or face imprisonment. Zimbabwe's courts tried to intervene. They again ruled the land seizures illegal. Mugabe responded by forcing the judges to resign and replacing them with cronies from his own party.

Because it could no longer produce enough food to feed its population, Zimbabwe had become dependent on foreign food aid. Mugabe used this aid as a weapon, rewarding his loyalists and preventing his opponents from receiving it. Just as he had done in Matabeleland in the 1980s, he used the threat of starvation to put down the people he suspected might oppose him. In particular, anyone suspected of being an MDC supporter was denied access to the vital staple crop, maize (corn). In the past, only war veterans, youth militia, and senior ZANU-PF officials had used this tactic. After the 2002 elections, it became more widespread, with "headmasters [school principals], businessmen, chiefs, and traditional leadership" using access to food for political ends.

A ZIMBABWEAN WOMAN HOLDS food she received from the Red Cross, an aid organization.

Most citizens who possessed skills and higher education abandoned Zimbabwe. So many trained medical personnel departed that the state health system collapsed. In total, about one-third of the entire population fled the country. The great majority of those who remained lived a miserable life. Only the elite leaders still loyal to Mugabe prospered.

In 2004 Mugabe cut off another source of potential criticism of his government. The ZANU-PF–dominated Parliament passed the Non-governmental Organizations Act. According to this act, foreign funding of local Zimbabwean human rights organizations became illegal. The act also banned foreign human rights organizations from operating inside the country.

The year 2005 witnessed another parliamentary election. For the preceding five years, Mugabe had directed the secret police and the regular police, the army, and the special youth brigades in campaigns against the opposition movement, the MDC. Meanwhile, the nation continued to experience record inflation—the highest in the world—and record economic collapse. The value of a Zimbabwe dollar showed the effect of this inflation. In 1980, the year of independence, a Zimbabwe dollar was worth more than one U.S. dollar. By the end of 2005 it was worth one-thousandth of a penny. The price of essential foods—maize, meat, milk, and bread—skyrocketed. The government responded by trying to control prices. As a result, a black market (the illegal trade of goods) sprang up and pushed prices ever higher.

A CLEAR SIGN

One sign of Zimbabwe's economic collapse came at the Harare Agricultural Show. Ever since 1895, farmers had brought large numbers of cattle, goats, sheep, chickens, and other animals to compete for prizes for the best livestock. It was a sign of how productive the land could be. In 2004, however, there were only nine head of cattle, two goats, and three sheep on display.

In the 2005 parliamentary elections, Mugabe again resorted to tactics of intimidation, violence, rape, torture, and murder. One new ploy was to deny the right to vote for thousands of Zimbabweans who had fled the country and were living elsewhere. Mugabe's ZANU-PF party gained a wider margin in Parliament over the rival MDC. On its website, the MDC denounced the election as a fraud. Neutral observers agreed. Mugabe's youth brigades, referred to by Zimbabweans as the "green bombers" because of their green uniforms, had been particularly intimidating to opponents of the government. Nonetheless, ZANU-PF now held a two-thirds majority, which allowed the president to change the constitution again so that Mugabe could run for yet another term as president. However, Mugabe said he would retire in 2007.

Following the March 2005 election, Mugabe skillfully divided and weakened his major political foe, the MDC. In yet another Mugabe-instigated constitutional amendment, a new chamber of Parliament was created, called the Senate. Some of the Senate seats were guaranteed to Mugabe loyalists. Whether to compete for the other seats was a question that

GREEN BOMBERS MARCH IN A parade celebrating Mugabe's birthday, shortly before the 2005 elections.

> *The symbolic gesture of support for ZANU-PF is a clenched fist. The MDC gesture is an open hand. An American visitor to Zimbabwe in 2005 caused panic among his hosts when he stretched his open hand out of their car window to feel the breeze. They feared being observed by ZANU-PF thugs, who would see it as a gesture of support for MDC. Similar gestures had resulted in severe beatings.*

caused the MDC to split into rival factions. Some in the party decided that the only way to have influence was by cooperating in the Senate election. This faction used government media to attack their former leader, Morgan Tsvangirai, who opposed cooperation. Others decided to remain a true opposition party and boycott the Senate election. In sum, Mugabe's ploy worked brilliantly because the split in the MDC weakened opposition to Mugabe's ZANU-PF.

Two months later, the government launched Operation Murambatsvina ("clear the filth"). This campaign was directed against poor Zimbabweans who lived in urban shantytowns (slums) throughout the nation. Many of these poor were families already devastated by the AIDS pandemic. The army and police evicted men, women, and children from their homes and then demolished the structures. Estimates of the number of people rendered homeless ranged from 300,000 to more than 1,000,000. The government did nothing to provide for them afterward.

TOP: ZIMBABWEAN POLICE DEMOLISH HOUSES ON THE OUTSKIRTS OF Harare in May 2005 as part of Operation Murambatsvina. *Bottom:* A woman and children amid the rubble created by Operation Murambatsvina in June 2005

An American visitor reported seeing crowds of newly homeless people wandering the streets of Harare's poorest neighborhood. The family she was visiting sheltered homeless people in their garage. The United Nations estimated that 7 percent of the nation's population were victims of Operation Murambatsvina. A white Zimbabwean human rights activist reported from Harare, "There's just complete shock in Zimbabwe. People didn't believe the government would go this far."

Mugabe's government claimed that this operation was a first step in a long-term plan to clean up urban areas, end crime, and restore order and dignity. Outside observers believed it was a government attempt to suppress potential urban unrest directed against the government. The Africa director of Human Rights Watch reported, "The Zimbabwean government has created a humanitarian crisis in which hundreds of thousands of people are now living without food, water, or shelter." Because the international community criticized Operation Murambatsvina, the Zimbabwean government blocked international humanitarian efforts to assist the displaced (people who have been forced to leave their homes).

In May 2006, Operation Murambatsvina resumed with a massive, monthlong roundup of some 10,000 people in the nation's capital. The official government media claimed that those arrested were criminals and that they would eventually be relocated. There was no information about how and where they were being held.

CHAPTER 5

INSTITUTI

IN 2005 ZIMBABWE'S POPULATION was estimated at 12,800,000. The Shona people make up about 75 percent of the population and the Ndebele about 20 percent. Other African people comprise most of the remaining population. The number of white people has been reduced to fewer than 50,000—from a peak of about 270,000 in 1975—as the government has moved to drive them out of Zimbabwe. There is also a small Asian population.

About four of every five people live outside the urban areas. Two-thirds of the urban dwellers live either in the capital, Harare, or the southwestern city of Bulawayo. Three-fourths of the population are Christian, a legacy of contact with Europeans and the establishment of missions and mission schools.

With a population that lives mostly in the countryside, institutions such as the media (to encourage and maintain communica-

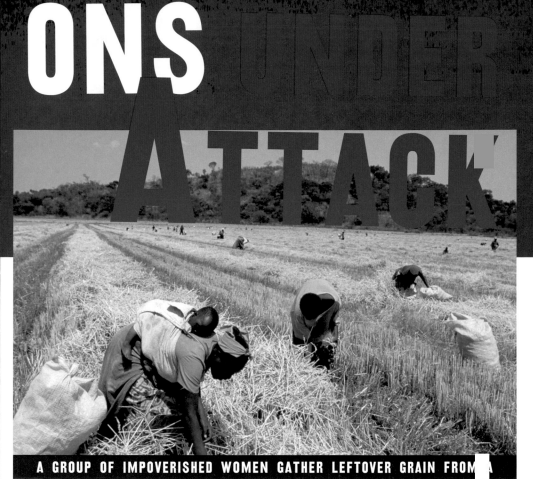

ONS UNDER ATTACK

A GROUP OF IMPOVERISHED WOMEN GATHER LEFTOVER GRAIN FROM A recent harvest to make porridge for their families. The majority of people in Zimbabwe live in rural areas and depend on agriculture to survive.

tion) and the government and court systems (to maintain law and order) are essential. But in Zimbabwe, these institutions are yet another means by which Mugabe wields his power.

THE MEDIA

In modern society, a free press serves as watchdog. Journalists serve the public by detecting and reporting on abuse and corruption in government and the private sector. Because a free press can challenge the absolute rule of a government, some governments clamp down on the press. So it was after Rhodesia declared its independence from British colonial rule. The government of Ian Smith passed numerous restrictive laws to control the press. For example, it was illegal for radio stations to play music whose lyrics were considered to be antigovernment. When Zimbabwe became independent in 1980, Mugabe retained most of these restrictions. For instance, radio announcers at the Zimbabwe Broadcast Company have to allow government officials to check their selections against a list of approved music before each broadcast. This is one among many of the ways Mugabe has used laws that white rulers once used to repress his own people.

When Zimbabwe became independent, it had both official state-controlled media outlets (newspapers, magazines, and radio and television stations) and independent newspapers. The state-controlled television stations and newspapers reported only what the government dictated, while independent newspapers reported news that showed the government in an unfavorable light or openly criticized the government. For example, independent newspapers uncovered and reported instances of government corruption. In one case, a Bulawayo newspaper pointed out the discrepancy between the wealth of ZANU-PF party officials and the poverty of war veterans. In response to such reports, the government promised to investigate, but did nothing.

As time passed, Mugabe decided not to tolerate any sort of public criticism. His government steadily restricted press freedom.

Parliament enacted laws controlling who can operate a media outlet and who can practice journalism. It used these laws to threaten and arrest those who criticize the government. Government-backed thugs seized and beat editors and bombed independent newspaper offices. When this failed to completely silence the independent media, the government enacted more restrictive laws to close down the independent newspapers. This behavior violates international principles of freedom of expression.

> *The government allows few foreign reporters inside the country. This is another means by which Mugabe keeps outsiders from knowing about the conditions in Zimbabwe.*

The year 1999 saw the establishment of what would become Zimbabwe's last independent newspaper, the *Daily News*. The *Daily News* published outspoken criticism of Mugabe. In response, Mugabe loyalists bombed the paper's printing presses. The police threatened and detained the paper's executives and reporters. Then, in preparation for the election of 2002, Parliament passed several Mugabe-supported acts designed to silence political opponents. The Public Order and Security Act established prison terms for anyone who promoted "hostility" toward the president. Later came the Access to Information and Protection of Privacy Act. Its title was misleading. In fact, the act required all media to register with the government. The government refused to allow independent media outlets to register, and then prosecuted and banned them for failing to register. The *Daily News* was ensnared in this unsolvable dilemma, and the government forced it to close in 2003. Independent radio and television stations are required to purchase exorbitantly priced broadcasting licenses. Only one independent television station exists in Zimbabwe, but it is off the air because the government will not give it airtime. As a result, only government-controlled stations operate inside Zimbabwe.

The *Daily News* has tried to fight in court for the right to continue publishing in Zimbabwe. The case worked its way through the courts for two years. The High Court ruled that banning the newspaper was illegal. In July 2005, Zimbabwe's Media and Information Commission ignored the court's decision and continued to ban the *Daily News.* The newspaper's editor said he was not surprised by the government's action but he had "not lost hope." Someday, he predicted, Mugabe and his party would be ousted.

Meanwhile, the *Daily News* managed to host a website in neighboring South Africa where, well into the 2000s, it continued to publish an on-line edition. The Zimbabwean minister of state for Information and

A POLICE OFFICER GUARDS the entrance to the *Daily News* the day after police raided its offices and closed it for operating illegally.

Publicity reacted to the online edition with this comment: "If they want to go and set up a website in Timbuktu or in Mars, they are welcome to do so and must take all their unaccredited journalists with them." His comment was an obvious threat of arrest aimed at any *Daily News* reporters who continued to work in Zimbabwe.

By enacting restrictive media laws, Mugabe has tried to ensure that the only voice Zimbabweans hear is the party voice of ZANU-PF. Yet an underground media movement within Zimbabwe has organized. Its reporters operate secretly and smuggle their stories to the outside world, typically by using the Internet. The London-based Institute for War and Peace Reporting supports these reporters by hosting a website for them and providing additional help. The worldwide growth of the Internet during the 1990s has allowed oppressed people around the world to write about life inside their countries and to read about life in the wider world.

A JOURNALIST READS A SPECIAL EDITION OF THE *DAILY NEWS* PRINTED IN Nigeria. Many of Zimbabwe's independent newspapers have had to move out of Zimbabwe because they are critical of Mugabe's government.

Zimbabweans have been able to outflank their censored news media by establishing dozens of websites.

Aware of the power of the electronic media, Mugabe's government passed a law in 2001 that allowed the state to secretly monitor anyone's e-mails. The High Court declared the law unconstitutional in 2004. The government quickly responded by passing a new law that made it illegal to use the Internet to criticize the government. Violators face arrest and payment of a fine. The government expects Internet service providers to take on the task of e-mail surveillance, but it is clearly impossible for any group to check every e-mail for antigovernment content.

Zimbabweans in exile and foreign journalists have created a number of websites to report accurately on events inside Zimbabwe. People living in Zimbabwe also continue to post reports on the Internet. Several of these sites were consulted for this book and are listed in Further Reading and Websites (p. 152).

It is unclear who is winning the battle to control Zimbabwe's media. Human Rights Watch has reported that the crackdown on the press is intensifying. The Africa director of Human Rights Watch has said, "The Zimbabwean government is using criminal charges to muzzle independent reporting and criticism."

THE GOVERNMENT AND THE COURTS

In preparation for its birth as an independent, majority-ruled nation, Zimbabwe ratified a constitution in 1979. By the terms of the constitution, Zimbabwe's government was organized under a parliamentary system, with three branches: executive, legislative, and judicial. The framers of the constitution intended that the three branches serve to check and balance one another so that no one branch became too powerful.

Zimbabwe's executive branch was first headed by Mugabe, as its prime minister, until the legislature declared Mugabe president in 1987 and granted him far-reaching executive power. The president is considered to be the head of state and the head of the government. Presidential elections occur every six years. But Mugabe has changed the laws whenever necessary so that there is no limit on the number of times he may run for reelection.

The nation's legislature, called Parliament, has 150 members. The president supervises the selection of 30 of the members, and voters elect the remaining 120. Parliamentary elections take place every five years. Whichever political party has a majority of the seats in Parliament can dominate the nation's lawmaking. Since its independence in 1980, Zimbabwe has had several parties competing for seats in Parliament. However, Mugabe and his party have openly declared their intention to run Zimbabwe as a single-party Communist state and have condemned all opposition parties and candidates. Mugabe's party has controlled Zimbabwe's Parliament since independence.

The ruling political party—Zimbabwe African National Union-Patriotic Front (ZANU-PF)—is in turn ruled by the politburo, like that of the former Soviet Union. The politburo is a council whose twenty-six members are appointed by the president. It ranks even higher than the president's cabinet. The national government also controls the appointment of people to other high-level positions—in the civil service, the police, and the military.

The judicial branch is organized like a pyramid, with numerous local courts at the base, courts of appeal on the next level, and the High Court, presided over by a chief justice, at the top of the pyramid. The president appoints the High Court's justices.

The original constitution of Zimbabwe had a Bill of Rights that could not easily be amended (changed). Mugabe has been able to bypass the constitution by directing Parliament to pass laws limiting freedom and civil rights.

When Mugabe first came to power, the judicial system acted as an independent check against official abuse. By the terms of the 1979 Lancaster House Agreement, Mugabe could not make constitutional changes until 1990. As soon as he was able, he reigned in the independent authority of the judiciary. He ignored court rulings

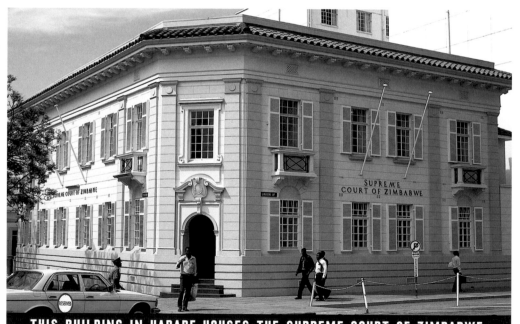

THIS BUILDING IN HARARE HOUSES THE SUPREME COURT OF ZIMBABWE.
Although the constitution gives courts independent authority, they have been ineffective in battling Mugabe.

SILENCING A CRITIC

One example among many of how Mugabe-run courts failed to protect civil rights in Zimbabwe occurred in 1999. In that year, the military arrested Mark Chavunduka, editor of the *Zimbabwe Standard*. He was held and tortured for nine days. During this time, his paper, and human rights activists around the world, appealed for his release. The court ruled his detention illegal but, Chavunduka later wrote, "Because the state chooses which judgments to respect and which to ignore, a mockery is being made of the entire judicial system. In my own case . . . the government ignored three orders from the Supreme Court that were issued within a space of five days, ordering my release from military custody." (Chavunduka died in 2002.)

he did not like and replaced judges with his cronies. When judges have made rulings that go against Mugabe's wishes, his government has ignored the rulings, and some judges have been forced to resign. Thus, in Zimbabwe, the president's power is no longer balanced by that of an independent judiciary.

Following the 2002 elections, a prominent ZANU-PF official publicly said that the government would not respect the rulings of the court if they interfered with what the government wanted to do. In the early twenty-first century, the court system continued to fail to protect the Zimbabwean people from the government. Instead, it was a government tool to control the people.

BY CONTROLLING INFORMATION AND WEALTH, a dictator retains control of a nation. Propaganda is the spreading of ideas, information, or rumors for the purpose of helping or, in some cases, injuring, an institution, a cause, or a person. It is the manipulation of public opinion. For example, dictators usually spread false information about themselves and their personal history, to make them appear more educated, heroic, and worthy of their leadership position. Government censorship seeks to stifle the spread of information or the expression of beliefs that contradict what the dictator wants people to believe. Dictators use the nation's wealth to buy personal loyalty and cooperation from people who can help keep the government in power. Finally, by pursuing influence in other nations, dictators try to prevent outsiders from coming to the aid of oppressed citizens.

OF A
DICTATOR

PROPAGANDA

Mugabe's government manipulates public opinion within and out-side of Zimbabwe's borders. It uses everything from biased reporting to outright lies, and it tries to isolate Zimbabweans from other sources of information. From the earliest days of his regime, Mugabe has incited Zimbabweans to suspect the former colonial powers of working against them. When not stirring up fears of British plots, he claimed that Joshua Nkomo of the rival ZAPU party was leading an army to overthrow him.

During the 2000 election campaign, government-controlled media outlets reported that the British navy was causing Zimbabwe's oil shortage by intercepting oil shipments. In addition, media outlets falsely claimed that British forces had gathered across the border in Botswana to invade the country and overthrow Mugabe. This propaganda was a blatant attempt to scare Zimbabweans into voting for Mugabe.

When the people of other nations hear about the hardships endured by Zimbabweans, Mugabe's government either blames the West or denies that a problem exists. For example, in 2005 international charity groups tried to provide assistance to thousands of poor and displaced Zimbabweans. The government blocked their efforts, and Bright Matonga, the deputy minister of information in

NO ONE IS SAFE

Even government officials and members of the ruling party can fall out of favor at any time. In July 2006, deputy information minister Bright Matonga was arrested as part of the government's drive to make an appearance of fighting corruption. The charges against him related to his previous post as head of the government-owned bus company. He was accused of asking for a bribe in exchange for awarding a contract to a bus supplier. Matonga denied the accusations and was released on bail. Observers outside of Zimbabwe believe that such arrests serve mainly to sow fear among government officials who might be thinking of challenging Mugabe's leadership.

the government's Propaganda Ministry, said that such groups were "creating a crisis that does not exist."

Mugabe's government also manipulates information by staging events that show him in a favorable light and having them publicized. For example, his party operatives use threats to coerce people into attending pro-Mugabe rallies. The rallies are then filmed by media outlets and broadcast to the people of Zimbabwe and other nations. This gives the false impression that Mugabe has the full support and affection of Zimbabweans.

PATRONAGE

Dictators possess power and can use that power for their own gain. Many dictators grow very rich while in power by helping themselves to government money or by confiscating property. They can use their wealth to help their supporters. This practice is called patronage, the power to appoint someone to an office or to give favors based on loyalty, not skill. Mugabe has used patronage both to reward his loyal supporters and to bribe potential foes.

Since the beginning of his reign, Mugabe has expanded the number of government jobs. These jobs go to ZANU-PF party members. The best government jobs are reserved for party leaders. In Zimbabwe, 80 percent of the people are unemployed. In such conditions, Mugabe's ability to offer paying jobs is a powerful tool to create support for his rule.

Land ownership is another powerful tool of patronage in Mugabe's Zimbabwe. When the government first began to seize white-owned commercial farms, Zimbabweans expected that the land would be distributed fairly to all the people. Instead the government rewarded many of its high-ranking loyalists by giving them the best farms. In later rounds of evictions, thousands of black peasants were evicted from land that they had cultivated since 2000. Mugabe then gave the land to black commercial farmers aligned with ZANU-PF.

All dictators know that they must keep their armed forces happy. Otherwise they risk being overthrown. The late Zimbabwean newspaper editor Mark Chavunduka once explained, "There's no doubt that the top ranks in the army have benefitted immensely from Mugabe's patronage." In particular, when Zimbabwean forces entered the Democratic Republic of Congo (DRC) in 1998, Mugabe allowed army officers to plunder. Chavunduka described how this worked: "You have a situation where, as soon as they get into the DRC on military operations, the top brass of the army make a beeline to go and concentrate on their private business interests." Officers instructed their men to steal equipment from mines and farms. They then used military transports to haul the stolen goods back to their own properties in Zimbabwe. Chavunduka concluded, "They [the soldiers] are the people who are really benefitting from Mugabe's patronage system."

Government corruption is a fact of life for everyday Zimbabweans. For example, managers of the state-run oil company had siphoned off so much money that the company could no longer pay its suppliers. As a result, people had to wait in lines all day to buy whatever fuel was available. Most available fuel was given to party officials and loyalists. As the gulf widened between wealthy government officials and hungry, unemployed Zimbabweans, the government realized it had to appear to be doing something about corruption if it wanted to claim it had any

PAUL MANGWANA'S PROMISES OF CURBING CORRUPTION HAVE SO FAR gone unfulfilled.

popular support. So Parliament passed an anticorruption act in January 2005, which created an anticorruption commission and the new government Ministry of State Enterprises, Anti-Corruption, and Anti-Monopolies. Prosecutions under the new act targeted only people whom the government viewed as disloyal. In December 2005, Paul Mangwana, the head of the ministry, announced that "the government was making its systems water-tight to curb corruption." Given that the new anticorruption com-mission included only Mugabe appointees chosen from among ZANU-PF loyalists, it is doubtful that any of these steps will yield results.

FOREIGN RELATIONS

Zimbabwe became an independent nation during the height of the Cold War (1945–1991), the worldwide struggle between Communist and democratic governments. The rival leaders of those nations, particularly the Soviet Union and China on the Communist side and the United States on the democratic side, often used African nations as pawns for their own ends. To avoid being used in this way, many smaller nations sought to remain neutral in the struggle between the superpowers. They formed the Non-Aligned Movement and began holding meetings in 1961. Zimbabwe, like other member nations of the Non-Aligned Movement, fell under suspicion of not being truly neutral in regard to Cold War politics.

Zimbabwe's foreign affairs also were driven by the nation's history of colonialism. Rhodesia had been a member of the Commonwealth of Nations. The commonwealth is an association of independent nations—almost all of which have been part of the

The United States was the first foreign country to establish an embassy in Zimbabwe, opening its embassy in Harare on April 18, 1980, Zimbabwe's first day of independence.

British Empire—whose main goal is to encourage economic cooperation among its members. It also promotes democracy, human rights, and good governance. At independence Zimbabwe became part of this organization, and as a member, the nation enjoyed economic benefits. As Mugabe steadily increased his dictatorial power and suppressed human rights and democratic institutions, he became at odds with the commonwealth. The commonwealth tried to persuade Mugabe to moderate his behavior, but these efforts failed.

Tensions reached a climax in 2002. Because of Mugabe's fraudulent election that year, the commonwealth suspended Zimbabwe from its annual meetings for one year. In December 2003, the commonwealth renewed its suspension. Mugabe responded by withdrawing from the commonwealth, a largely symbolic gesture, since the commonwealth has no real power over its members. However, Mugabe's withdrawal potentially cut him off from some sources of foreign aid.

Zimbabwe also had a long history of opposition to South Africa's white supremacist, or apartheid, policies and of support for Namibia's freedom from South Africa. South Africa had supported Ian Smith's regime against Mugabe's guerrillas. Thus it was not surprising that Mugabe spoke out against South Africa's apartheid government. However, while publicly supporting democratic change to black majority rule in South Africa, Mugabe would not allow antiapartheid guerrillas to establish bases inside Zimbabwe. In this way, Mugabe cleverly maintained his role as champion of black nationalism while minimizing the risk of attack from South Africa's pro-apartheid government forces.

The most puzzling aspect of Zimbabwean foreign policy came in 1998, when Mugabe sent his military to intervene in the civil war in the Congo. This intervention proved enormously costly for the already struggling Zimbabwean economy. Whether it was a calculated move to distract attention from internal difficulties (a classic ploy used by dictators) or simply an unwise strategy remains unknown. What is certain is that the Zimbabwean military was allowed to use the intervention for personal gain.

Mugabe's Congo intervention cost Zimbabwe $1,000,000 a day for four years to keep 11,000 soldiers in the Congo. For a huge profit, the Congo granted a Mugabe-controlled company the right to cut down 84,000,000 acres (34,000,000 hectares) of rain forest, 15 percent of the Congo's entire land area.

Western nations have imposed a variety of sanctions against Zimbabwe. For example, in reaction to Zimbabwe's rigged election of 2002, the United States and the European Union banned senior Zimbabwean officials from entering their nations, limited sales of military weapons to Zimbabwe, and froze the overseas financial assets of selected Zimbabwean officials. The Western countries suspected that these assets had been obtained illegally and hoped to use this maneuver to pressure Zimbabwe toward reform. Following the rigged elections of 2005, the United States blocked access to additional financial assets in the United States held by 128 individuals and thirty-three Zimbabwean institutions closely linked to Mugabe and his associates.

International sanctions have had limited success, however, in large part because Zimbabwe receives political and economic support from some of its fellow African leaders. Mugabe remains a powerful symbol of black African independence and for that reason continues to appeal to African nationalists. For example, when Zimbabwe celebrated its twenty-fifth year of independence, the anonymous writer of a website based in Ghana praised Mugabe with these words: "Firm, resilient, and undeterred are just some of the characteristics of Africa's leading leader. Never mind the relentless attacks by the world wide media machine, Zimbabwe's president, Robert Gabriel Mugabe remains the most respected leader on the continent."

Most important, just as the white South African government supported Ian Smith's white Rhodesian government, so the black South African government of Thabo Mbeki supports Mugabe into the early twenty-first century. In November 2005, the intelligence ministers of South Africa and Zimbabwe met to sign an agreement of cooperation on security and defense. Zimbabwean officials claim that South Africa has agreed to share information on nongovernmental organizations, such as human rights organizations, that oppose Mugabe. Outside observers believe that this agreement is designed to help Mugabe crush his foes.

Because the common people of Zimbabwe have suffered greatly under Mugabe over the past decades, charitable organizations and foreign governments worldwide have tried to help relieve the suffering. However, beginning at least with the first campaign into

SOUTH AFRICA AND ZIMBABWE: THE FLOW OF INFORMATION AND PEOPLE

When Robert Mugabe became prime minister of Zimbabwe in 1980, many white Zimbabweans fled to South Africa. Since the South African government controlled that nation's press, newly independent Zimbabwe provided a haven for journalists reporting on South Africa, which was still under apartheid.

A decade later, white rule and apartheid ended in South Africa, and in 1994 Nelson Mandela became the nation's first black president. During that time, the Zimbabwean government had assumed increasing control over its own press and population. Journalists began leaving Zimbabwe for South Africa, where they could report freely. As survival has grown more difficult in Zimbabwe, the trickle of emigration to South Africa—by both black and white people—has become a flood *(below)*. Many Zimbabweans have family members or friends living in South Africa.

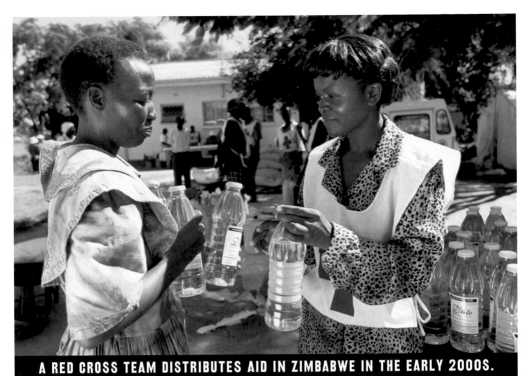

A RED CROSS TEAM DISTRIBUTES AID IN ZIMBABWE IN THE EARLY 2000S.
Drought combined with political mismanagement has left many Zimbabweans suffering from food and water shortages.

Matabeleland in the 1980s, Mugabe's government has used food donations and foreign aid as a weapon. It withholds them from its enemies and gives them only to party loyalists. For example, in 2002, Oxfam Canada (a human rights organization) reported that Zimbabwe's state-run Grain Marketing Board was the only Mugabe-approved source for the public to purchase maize. Yet Mugabe allowed the board to sell the maize only to members of the ruling ZANU-PF party.

A pattern has emerged in Zimbabwe's history of foreign relations. As Mugabe's rule grew increasingly dictatorial, most of the international community reacted with growing criticism. Mugabe in turn responded to such criticism by tightening his control over the nation. By restricting travel, he has limited or eliminated the ability of foreigners, especially international human rights organizations, to see what is happening inside Zimbabwe. The ability of his critics to use the Internet to spread word about the horrors of his regime has been one of the few checks against his control. Mugabe continues his effort to block this ability.

CENSORSHIP

Zimbabweans cannot openly turn to the arts, entertainment, or music to find relief from their struggles, because the government controls the production of these activities. In the past, Zimbabwe enjoyed a rich musical tradition. During the struggle for independence, musicians composed songs dedicated to black nationalist guerrillas. The Ian Smith government passed a Censorship and Entertainment Control Act in 1967 to limit free artistic expression. With little change, this law still applies in modern Zimbabwe.

For example, the Zimbabwe Board of Censors is empowered "to make such inquiries as it may consider necessary in regard to any publication, picture, statue, record, or public entertainment." All that is required for the Board of Censors to interfere is for someone to claim that a book or record is antigovernment. The consequence of this sweeping power is that artists, writers, and performers in Zimbabwe work in a climate of fear and intimidation. As a result, some have fled Zimbabwe, but it is impossible to know exactly how many.

On May 1, 2006—a traditional day of international celebration for Communists—Hosiah Chipanga, a prominent Zimbabwean musician, intended to take part in a workers' march. Chipanga composes songs that accurately describe conditions in Zimbabwe. He withdrew from the march after receiving death threats over the phone. The previous year, Chipanga pulled out of a concert after being threatened by the secret police. In this way, Mugabe's thugs had silenced yet another Zimbabwean voice.

AT THE DAWN OF INDEPENDENCE, Zimbabweans hoped to enjoy greater freedom, access to education and jobs, better health care, and the opportunity to own better farmland than they had under Rhodesia's white supremacist government. Mugabe has dashed every one of these hopes through deliberate policy, mismanagement of the national economy, and corruption on a massive scale.

CURBS ON FREEDOM

Under Mugabe the people of Zimbabwe live in the absence of democratic rights. A Zimbabwean human rights activist who is also a nurse has been treating displaced Zimbabweans (those who have

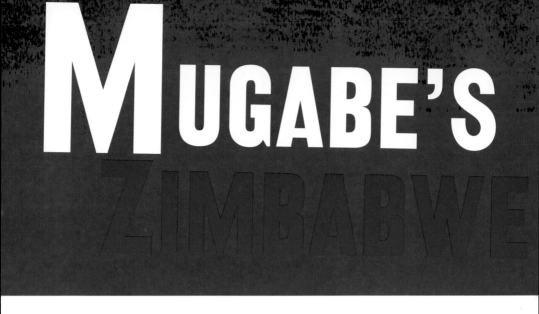

MUGABE'S ZIMBABWE

been forced to leave their homes) since 2002. She reports that the government has apparently adopted torture as its preferred means of controlling the population. Common citizens face "beatings, branding and cutting, electrocution, partial drowning, rape and sexual torture."

Elections are rigged through the use of political violence and intimidation. The judiciary is controlled by ZANU-PF, and the police follow the government's orders. Consequently, the rule of law does not protect citizens. The government does not protect minority rights. In particular, it continues to take land from the remaining white farmers. Parliament has passed repressive laws aimed at preventing freedom of speech and association. Even free travel is restricted. The constitution allows the government to take away the passports of anyone who criticizes the government.

TORTURE

The word *torture* appears many times in this book. A word can lose its meaning when it is read over and over. Common examples of torture in Zimbabwe include the following two cases:

- Over a period of three days, torturers hung a human rights lawyer upside down for hours at a time, and the police delivered strong electric shocks to his feet, mouth, and genitals.
- Torturers held the heads of opposition party members under water until they were at the point of drowning, then revived them and did it again and again.

Freedom of assembly does not exist. The Public Order and Security Act of 2002 makes it a crime to hold a public gathering without giving the police four days' written notice. Whenever groups gather publicly, government watchers also attend. Among many examples, in 2005 labor leaders conducted a peaceful protest against poverty. Police seized the leaders and imprisoned them. Many were tortured while in prison. Amnesty International reports, "The government [continues] its campaign of repression aimed at eliminating political opposition and silencing dissent. Hundreds of people [have been] arrested for holding meetings or participating in peaceful protests. The police, army, supporters of the ruling Zimbabwe African National Union-Patriotic Front (ZANU-PF) and youth militia [are] implicated in numerous human rights violations, including torture, assault and arbitrary detention."

A POLICEMAN TRIES TO BLOCK A GROUP OF MEN PROTESTING TORTURE,
school fees, and lack of AIDS medications in Harare in December 2006.

JOBS

During Mugabe's reign, economic hardship has dominated the daily life of most everyone in Zimbabwe. Yet when Zimbabwe became an independent nation in 1980, few suspected that this would be so. Independence and majority rule offered the African people of Zimbabwe their first chance in nearly a century to enjoy the abundance of their land. They aspired to economic advancement and better lives. The end of war also gave families the joy of welcoming home from the war their long-absent loved ones.

During the first decade of his rule, Mugabe more or less observed the Lancaster House Agreement of 1979. This agreement limited his ability to violate the rule of law and civil society.

Consequently, most Zimbabweans enjoyed some increase in prosperity. In 1990 a Zimbabwean observed, "only the whites used to have nice and prosperous things. We used to think that only the white man could have water in his house or in the yard. . . . [T]oday things are different . . . many of us now have cars. . . . It was only after the war that people began to understand that they had rights and how to do constructive jobs to raise the standards of their lives."

Prior to Zimbabwean independence, the rural black African population (about 4,000,000 in 1980) had been restricted to the 40,000,000 acres (16,200,000 hectares) of arid lands called Communal Areas. Overcrowding, overgrazing, and neglect had degraded the ability of this land to support its population. Another 500,000 rural Africans worked as laborers for white farmers, and many continued to do so after independence. Typically the black African laborers were housed

BEFORE INDEPENDENCE MANY BLACK ZIMBABWEANS WERE FORCED TO live in Communal Areas such as this one in Marange District.

in crude huts with poor sanitation. They received weekly food rations, basic medical care, and minimal salaries.

After 1980 landowners still paid the laborers minimal wages but no longer provided food or medicine. A decade later, black farm laborers still subsisted at the bottom of the rural economy. In 1990 one laborer noted, "Life since independence has not changed very much for me. . . . The freedom fighters used to tell us that we would have plenty of land but I am still tilling my field and I haven't been given any more land. The same applies to everyone else."

Some experienced black farmers who had received formerly white-owned farmland became successful commercial farmers. Many others, however, lacked experience in large-scale farming. They produced only enough to survive and supplemented their food supply by hunting the game that roamed their acreage. A few benefited from training programs offered by the government's

In October 2005, the Institute for War and Peace Reporting wrote, "As [Zimbabwe's] economy continues to crumble, the poor have become poorer, with very few able to afford a decent meal a day." The institute noted that Zimbabwe's economy had been declining steeply for five years. It estimated that unemployment was 80 percent. In other words, eight of every ten adults could not find jobs.

TWO FORMERLY LANDLESS BLACKS HERD CATTLE ON A PREVIOUSLY WHITE-
owned farm northwest of Harare. Many blacks failed to be as productive on farms
as the previous white owners, either from inexperience or lack of financial backing.

Agricultural Extension Service. Reported a single mother of eleven children in 1990, "To accomplish my goal I decided to join an agriculture group. . . . Here we are taught better techniques of plowing and planting by extension workers. . . . I received a number of spare parts for a plow. . . . The parts helped me a great deal which is why my fields look good this year." However, such programs failed to reach or recruit a majority of rural blacks. In recent years, agricultural extension programs have been severely hampered by lack of funding.

Before 1980 a huge discrepancy existed between white and black incomes and employment. The white minority controlled the government and passed laws that barred black Africans from skilled jobs. Even black Africans employed as servants could not enter the cities unless they had official passes from their employers.

Independence brought large numbers of black Africans into the cities in search of jobs. Many succeeded in finding work in occupational fields formerly reserved for whites, such as the civil service, clerical, and banking fields. Blacks began rising to management positions. The new government funded skills-training programs and some skilled jobs opened up as whites emigrated. A new black elite, made up of those with educations and skills, moved into pleasant homes in the formerly all-white suburbs. Though blacks and whites lived side by side, most had little to do with one another. Many blacks continued to work as domestic servants for wealthy households of both races.

Although Mugabe's victory spurred thousands of white people to emigrate, many chose to remain in Zimbabwe because it was the only home they had known. They simply could not imagine living somewhere else. This was especially true of farmers, who were attached to the land on which they had grown up. Because of Mugabe's early promises of reconciliation, the white population, like the blacks, looked forward to better lives. No longer at war, no longer suffering from international sanctions, their fears of retribution laid to rest, many white Zimbabweans returned to their prewar lives of wealth and power. They continued to dominate the arenas of business and commercial farming. Some white Zimbabweans held onto their racist attitudes, while others embraced a more equal society led by majority rule.

Class distinctions did not disappear in independent Zimbabwe, however. Lower-income whites, for example, faced direct competition from a black population with new economic freedom. These whites faced a greater struggle to get by than they had under the white-dominated Rhodesian regime when blacks could work only as farm laborers or domestic servants. Some young whites began to believe they were the ones suffering from racial discrimination and began planning for their futures outside of Zimbabwe. During the first decade of independence, Zimbabwe's white population fell by half due to emigration, from about 200,000 to less than 100,000.

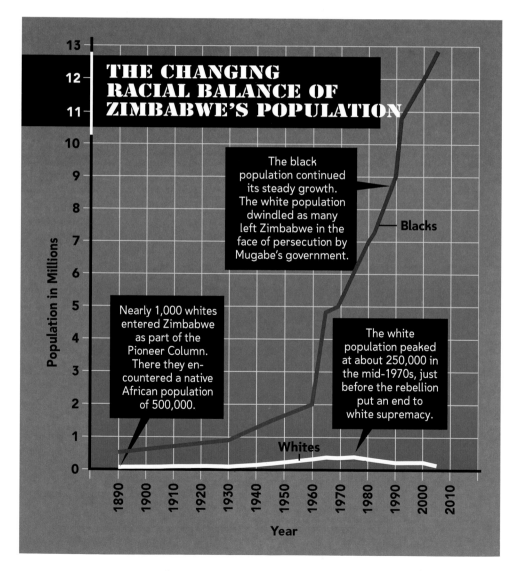

THE CHANGING RACIAL BALANCE OF ZIMBABWE'S POPULATION

The black population continued its steady growth. The white population dwindled as many left Zimbabwe in the face of persecution by Mugabe's government.

Blacks

Nearly 1,000 whites entered Zimbabwe as part of the Pioneer Column. There they encountered a native African population of 500,000.

The white population peaked at about 250,000 in the mid-1970s, just before the rebellion put an end to white supremacy.

Whites

Population in Millions

Year

Accompanying the devastating economic hardship is total poverty. The currency is nearly worthless, barely two people in ten have jobs, education and health care are unavailable to most, and an estimated three-fourths of the remaining population suffers from hunger. As the currency continues to plummet in value, each day sees uncontrolled increases in the prices of basic goods such as bread, placing them out of reach even for people with jobs. A professor at the University of Zimbabwe said, "Everything that could go wrong here is going wrong. The future will be bleaker and bleaker until the people of Zimbabwe say that they have nothing to lose but their pain, and that it's time to throw out the dictator."

THESE CHILDREN ARE STUDENTS at a mixed-race school in Zimbabwe. Schools were integrated at independence.

EDUCATION

Before 1980 white children received free public education, while black parents had to pay for their children's education, even at mission schools. At independence, Zimbabwe's schools were opened to children of all races. The new government increased spending on education in order to open new schools, train new teachers, and offer free primary education and low-cost secondary education to all. However, such rapid expansion caused the quality of public schools to deteriorate. By 1992 the goal of free education was abandoned and school fees rose out of reach for many. Many whites, joined by wealthy blacks, responded by sending their children to private schools. By law the private schools were no longer segregated as they had been under colonial and white rule. The younger children of both races learned to mingle freely and play together, while many older white children held on to their racial prejudices.

Upon independence Western nations lavished generous foreign aid on Zimbabwe. Mugabe spent some of the funds to improve health care and education for the black population. Since the new national army and police force could not absorb the thousands of former guerrillas, the government paid modest bonuses of a few thousand dollars apiece to the unemployed who had served with the nationalist military.

Some veterans used this money to acquire job training, education, or to start businesses or farming cooperatives. (Cooperatives are enterprises or organizations that are owned by and operated for the benefit of those using its services.) These enterprises met with mixed results. Other war veterans, many of whom had spent their childhoods at war and not in school, faced uncertain futures. Estimates indicate that nearly half of the veterans endured long periods of unemployment. A black Zimbabwean woman expressed her frustration in 1990: "My children cannot find employment. Indeed, many children who went to fight—not only my own—cannot find work. . . . Sometimes I think it is even worse than the period when the children were fighting. . . . I feel betrayed because many children who fought for this country have nothing to do."

The forerunner to the University of Zimbabwe had existed in Harare since 1957. A second university, the National University of

TWO STUDENTS WORK IN A laboratory at the University of Zimbabwe. The student population increased from around 2,000 in 1980 to more than 10,000 in 2000.

Science and Technology, was established in Bulawayo in 1991. A private Methodist university opened in Mutare in 1992. A number of technical and agricultural colleges also opened to serve Zimbabweans. The reformed school system released more literate and educated black Africans into the workforce than ever before in Zimbabwe's history. They had every reason to hope for and expect jobs that would permit them to use their skills.

However, the Mugabe government's disastrous mishandling of the economy led to runaway inflation and high unemployment. New graduates began to see their educations as futile. Unable to find work, unable to enjoy the promise of economic advancement, and mired in increasing poverty, the educated younger generation formed a dissatisfied population that fueled political opposition.

The nonprofit human rights agency Institute for War and Peace Reporting interviewed a squatter whose home was one of hundreds of thousands demolished by the government during Operation Murambatsvina in May 2005 and May 2006. The man's twenty-four-year-old son lived with him since he was unable to find a job. His sixteen-year-old daughter had just dropped out of school because he was unable to afford her continuing education. He feared that his youngest child, a twelve-year-old girl, would also be unable to finish school. His fears were not unusual. A United Nations envoy (representative) reported that Operation Murambatsvina had forced some 300,000 children to drop out of school.

The father worked at night as a security guard and during the day as a street vendor. Since street vending was illegal, the police frequently arrested him. However, the police did this in order to obtain bribes because they too had great difficulty making ends meet. On bad days, the father had to give up most of his earnings as bribes. On good days, he made enough to eat. The interview ended with the question, "And what are you going to have for lunch today?" The man responded, "A bun. I survived the police today."

A poor fifty-seven-year-old black man compared life before and after Mugabe's rise to power. He said, "Under Smith there was racism and segregation. But to be honest I think the quality of life was better. As a gardener, I used to eat bread every day. But under Mugabe things are really bad. I can't afford to buy bread."

In May 2006, a Harare reporter described the challenge of education for victims of Operation Murambatsvina. The reporter interviewed an eleven-year-old girl whose family's only source of income, a carpentry shop, had been demolished during the operation. Without money to pay school fees, the family relied on charity. When the charity ran out, the girl dropped out of school. The newspaper reporter found her sitting in the dirt studying an old English textbook. She was trying to teach four other younger children how to write by drawing their names in the dirt. She said, "I would like to go back to school soon and join my classmates." But first her parents needed to find a way to pay the fees. A local education official noted that school fees were rising as the entire nation experienced soaring inflation over 1,000 percent.

In another squatters' camp, a twelve-year-old girl had been unable to attend school for the past year. She lived in a shack with her grandmother and worked all day crushing stone to sell to builders.

WHO OWNS ZIMBABWE?

Mugabe initially treated white commercial farmers with great care. Their productive farms were vital to the national economy, and Zimbabwe needed the food and wealth they generated. Although Mugabe and his party were avowedly Communist, in the early days of the regime they appeared to accept that some degree of capitalist enterprise was necessary to keep the economy going. However, one-party Communism remained Mugabe's long-term goal, and the regime quickly moved to nationalize businesses and suppress political opposition.

As new members of the government and business elites pursued luxurious lifestyles, they turned to corruption to pay for them. Government officials took possession of businesses that had been nationalized and land and homes vacated by fleeing white people. They used their positions to loot the national treasury and enrich themselves. They left little in the treasury for the working people whom Communism was supposed to benefit.

Mugabe's policies and the corruption among members of his government ground down the economy. Foreign nations withdrew their financial assistance, and the Zimbabwe dollar plunged in value. Basic goods and food grew more expensive as production dropped. As farms and businesses closed, thousands of people lost their jobs. Job skills and education levels among black Zimbabweans had improved since 1980, but due to economic stagnation and unemployment most of the black population saw no long-term improvement in their standard of living.

While common people struggled as the economy got worse and food became more expensive, the independent press reported about official corruption. People continued to read stories about the new privileged class created by Mugabe's government. They read of Mugabe's extravagant personal spending and of cabinet ministers buying new cars, sending their children overseas to elite schools, and traveling to Europe. They could not help contrasting these stories with their own difficult lives. They resented wealthy blacks, but they especially resented whites, who appeared to be as privileged as ever. Mugabe continued to gain political support by stoking racial resentments. He promised the voters that he would take more land away from white farmers and give it to black Zimbabweans.

Many individual white farmers provided secure jobs, treated their employees well, and earned their respect. However, because of their obvious wealth—including fine houses and cars—white farmers were targets for black resentment. As Zimbabwe approached twenty years as an independent nation, Mugabe decided that his government would take white-owned land and pay nothing for it. He did this in part to punish the white population, whom he blamed for the strengthening political opposition in Zimbabwe. Mugabe then used the land to reward his supporters, while giving as little of it as possible to the people who needed it most. His campaign against white farmers grew more brutal with each passing year.

To put on a good face, the government arranged for several thousand poor rural black Africans to occupy white-owned farms in what became a media event in February 1998. The news media duly took note of the elated people who arrived on foot with bundles of belongings. An American reporter described several hundred people as they camped and built rough shelters on a white farmer's land, within sight of his spacious house and swimming pool and surrounded by sleek cattle grazing on lush pastures. They had marked out individual plots of land with sticks. Some said that the government had promised them this land, which was better than what they had before.

One woman happily told the reporter, "This is our land now. . . . We will be very happy here. The farmer can stay in his house, we will just grow mealies [corn] here."

The white farm owner appealed to the local police, who waited for instructions from the government. Two months later, having received the desired publicity, the government transported the squatters back to their former land, promising them new land later in the year.

This event was merely a chance for Mugabe to appear as the leader who bestowed land on his people. The farm occupations of the early twenty-first century were more serious. Mugabe designed them to intimidate the voters before the June 2000 parliamentary elections. Each series of farm invasions typically began at the fourteen-story ZANU-PF headquarters building in Harare. There young men assembled while waiting for their orders. Then they piled onto trucks that transported them to the targeted property.

For a white farmer and his family, the first warning would be a commotion at the gate—most had security fences around their

MANY WHITES HAD FARMWORKERS BUILD SECURITY FENCES AT THE END of white minority rule. These fences continue to protect white landowners from land invasion.

homes. It might take the form of a crowd shouting war slogans and beating drums, or it might be the sound of a truck crashing through the gate. In April 2000, a white farming couple and their son heard the mob crash through the gate and hid in an outbuilding. They listened to the sounds of the invaders wrecking their house, breaking their furniture, and ransacking their belongings in search of anything of value. The mob then found and stormed the family's hiding place. The phone lines had been cut, but the owner got a radio message out to his neighbors. Only the arrival of a posse of neighbors, accompanied by black laborers who had volunteered to help, prevented bloodshed. Days later the attackers returned and firebombed the house. The family fled to Harare.

A number of white farmers known to support Mugabe's opposition were marked for death. Police set up roadblocks to prevent neighbors from coming to their aid. One farmer reported watching from behind a police roadblock as his neighbor's house was set on fire and the neighbor was shot dead as he fled the burning house.

One evening in May 2000, on a farm near Harare, Alan Dunn was at home watching television with his wife and three daughters. Somebody knocked on the door. When Dunn answered it, unknown attackers dragged him out to his garage and beat him to death. Several of Dunn's black employees, who had tried to warn him of strangers in the area, respected him because he helped them by plowing their farm plots with his tractor and transporting their crops to market. They mourned his loss, saying that the invaders who had stolen the land would never help them like Dunn had.

Farm invasions did not stop with the white owners and their families. In August 2000, squatters abducted a group of black children from a school on a commercial farm. The gang took the children to their camp, forced them to chant pro-Mugabe slogans, and molested the girls. When the police arrived, they stood around and watched for several hours. The gang eventually released the children, but only in exchange for their parents. They then held the parents overnight and subjected them to beatings.

As time passed, citizens realized that Mugabe's promises for land reform were not working. The whites no longer controlled the land, but after they left, the land failed to produce. As early as 1994, an independent Zimbabwean newspaper revealed that many of the confiscated farms had been given to government officials—including the minister of agriculture—instead of to landless rural blacks. This proved the last straw for Great Britain, which had spent 44 million pounds (about 70 million U.S. dollars) subsidizing (providing money for) the land redistribution program. The British government withdrew its support.

Among the hundreds of thousands of Zimbabweans who have fled or been driven out are the white farmers. Of the 70,000 whites who had remained in Zimbabwe, an estimated 90 percent left the country after 2002. Most went to Australia, New Zealand, and Great

In August 2006, Mugabe moved into his new palace in a suburb of Harare. It boasts twenty-five bedrooms and an equal number of bathrooms, and cost the equivalent of twenty-six million U.S. dollars to build. He also has four other huge luxury homes in Zimbabwe.

Britain. Some found new homes in neighboring Mozambique. The government of Mozambique has actively recruited skilled white farmers to help build its economy. A prominent Mozambique sociologist explained, "A problem for Zimbabwe has become a solution for Mozambique."

HEALTH

Prior to independence, Zimbabwe's health care system was segregated and unequal in quality. The white health care system performed splendidly. The health of the white population rivaled that of people in prosperous Western nations. Health care for blacks was superior to that of many places in Africa but was still far below the quality of care that whites received. Certain key statistics underscored the differences. Among blacks in Zimbabwe, infant mortality was an estimated ten times greater than among whites. Unlike the white population, numerous black children suffered from malnutrition. Poor sanitation across the country caused contaminated water, which led to the spread of infectious diseases among the black population.

Upon independence Mugabe's government upgraded health care for the black population. It opened new rural clinics and began training additional medical personnel. While indicators of health, such as life expectancy, improved for blacks, too few health care facilities existed to serve the population. After a promising start at reform, waste and corruption at high levels of government left the national treasury unable to maintain the new facilities. In many government-funded hospitals, health care standards and proper sanitation were lacking and basic supplies were inadequate. As a result, wealthier whites and blacks turned to private facilities for their health care.

The AIDS pandemic has hit Zimbabwe hard. Sexual abuse in militia camps during the war for independence made the problem worse. Later, Mugabe's thugs used rape against male and female prisoners as a tool of intimidation and punishment. A twenty-five-year-old former member of Mugabe's youth militia was interviewed in 2004. He was dying of AIDS. He reported, "We would be sent out into the countryside to punish people who support the opposition. We would beat people and sometimes burn down their homes. Other times we were ordered to rape women who did not support the ruling party. If a militia member refused to do this,

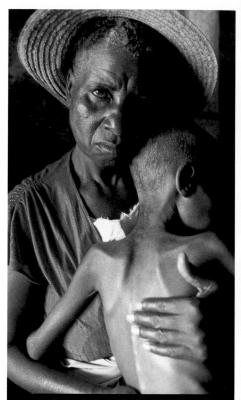

AIDS AFFECTS HUGE NUMBERS of people in Zimbabwe. This woman comforts her grandson, who is dying of AIDS-related diseases.

he himself would be raped." Unprotected sex caused an estimated HIV incidence as high as 40 percent within the militia. No one knows the incidence of HIV among their victims, although the country's overall level of infection is high.

Zimbabwe's population is an estimated 12,800,000 people. More than 2,000,000 people (about 15 percent) are living with HIV, the virus that causes AIDS, and 1,300,000 children have been orphaned by the disease. AIDS patients occupy 70 percent of hospital beds. Mostly because of AIDS, average life expectancy in Zimbabwe has fallen from about 62 years in 1990 to 37 years for men and 34 years for women in the early twenty-first century.

With underfunded treatment for HIV/AIDS, the government imposed an AIDS tax on wage-earning Zimbabweans. This money was to help pay for AIDS medicine. However, the price for the medicine continues to be too high for most citizens. Those suffering from HIV/AIDS have to depend on international aid, including special AIDS programs funded by the United States and by religious charities.

OUTSIDE OF HARARE, WOMEN LINE UP TO HAVE THEIR CHILDREN IMMUNIZED against measles. Most Zimbabweans struggle to provide health care for themselves and their families.

TRAVEL DIFFICULTIES

Fuel is in short supply in Zimbabwe because the economy can no longer generate enough money to import it. Local supplies are therefore limited. With little gasoline available, those who are fortunate enough to have jobs do not drive to work. Instead they walk miles each day to their jobs *(below)*. An American Baptist youth group traveled to Zimbabwe for a month in the early 2000s to visit schools and work with young students. They had planned to stay longer but could not obtain enough gasoline to fuel their vehicles. On one occasion, they spent nine hours at a fuel-

ing facility in Harare waiting for a fuel truck, which never arrived. On another occasion, their host spent the entire night waiting in vain for fuel. They witnessed the outbreak of a riot when a group of policemen, apparently drunk, arrived at the fueling station and began shoving and beating the waiting customers. The youth group was able to go on only one bus trip to another town. However, on the way, the driver had to stop every few miles at a police roadblock and pay a bribe to continue the journey.

By and large, these programs are able to function without interference from the Zimbabwean government. By working with local groups, these programs have slowed the spread of AIDS as well as other diseases such as malaria in Zimbabwe.

Nonetheless, Zimbabwe faces a health crisis because of its crumbling economy. The burden of providing for the nation's health care falls heavily on rural hospitals and clinics, because three-fourths of the population lives in rural areas. However, these providers face enormous problems. Procuring medicines is virtually impossible because Zimbabwe lacks the money to import them. Because the electricity supply is so erratic, power outages are frequent. Fuel to run backup generators is expensive and requires waiting in line for hours to buy it. Finding and retaining skilled health care personnel is particularly hard. Salaries are so low and the currency so worthless that doctors and nurses are fleeing Zimbabwe to make a living wage elsewhere.

Unemployment and inflation have robbed people of the ability to purchase basic health and hygiene goods. For example, feminine hygiene pads have become a luxury item in Zimbabwe that only the rich can afford. The average salary for the 20 percent of workers who have jobs is equal to twenty-one U.S. dollars per month. A month's supply of pads costs the equivalent of five U.S. dollars. So instead of spending one-fourth of their income on pads, women rely on substitutes—many of which are unhygienic and contribute to the spread of disease. A Zimbabwean trade group requested help from South Africa and Great Britain, both of which donated hygiene pads. However, Zimbabwean government border inspectors refused to allow the products into the country, claiming that they required quality testing. This kind of government interference adversely affects all aspects of daily life in Zimbabwe.

POLITICS AND GOVERNMENT IN MODERN ZIMBABWE are dominated by one man—Robert Mugabe. This kind of one-man rule is called autocratic rule. Elections are rigged and unfair. According to Lovemore Madhuku, chairman of a Zimbabwean pro-democracy group, "The regime is governing without the consent of the people—but many people have been intimidated into silence." Opposition members of Parliament are routinely harassed and threatened and often arrested. They frequently endure jail sentences and torture. Many Zimbabweans have fled the country, making new lives elsewhere. Meanwhile, Mugabe loyalists compete with one another to gain favor from their leader. They then use their positions for personal gain. Official corruption is a standard part of life in Zimbabwe. As Zimbabwean political scientist Eliphas Mukonoweshuro noted, "The difference between ordinary activities and crime has been very blurred."

ROBERT MUGABE, ESCORTED BY HIS BODY GUARDS, MAKES THE SYMBOLIC gesture of support for ZANU-PF, a clenched fist, as he walks toward a summit of Eastern and Southern African heads of state in the east African nation of Djibouti.

The Movement for Democratic Change has publicly pledged that it will continue the struggle for democratic change in Zimbabwe. In 2004 it initiated a program called RESTART (Reconstruction, Stabilization, Recovery, and Transformation), which identified crucial economic and service sectors that require rejuvenation. They include education, health, and agriculture. RESTART also asserted the need to develop a true democracy in Zimbabwe. However, while it is easy to identify problems, it can be very challenging to make concrete proposals about how to fix them.

In 2007 Mugabe turned eighty-three years old. He had been head of state for more than a quarter of a century. He had responded to all challenges to his government with ruthlessness and cruelty. His term of office was supposed to end in 2008; but in 2006, ZANU-PF postponed the 2008 presidential election until 2010. When Mugabe finally retires (which he has given no indication he will do) or dies, change will come to Zimbabwe. But dictators seldom take the risk of helping the nation prepare for life after they are gone. There are already rumors of leaders from ZANU-PF and MDC meeting in secret to plan what will happen after Mugabe's death. However, the government continues to pass laws to persecute its opponents. For example, in late 2005, the constitution was amended to permit confiscation of passports from people who criticize the regime and to forbid any recourse to the courts for people whose land has been seized.

At one time, Mugabe's powerful former intelligence chief, Emmerson Mnangagwa, was believed to be a possible replacement for Mugabe. However, Mnangagwa had not built a support base among the voting public. He owed his position to Mugabe's patronage. He has since been displaced by Joyce Mujuru, Zimbabwe's vice president since 2004. Mujuru fought in the war for independence while still in her teens, taking the name Teurai Ropa, which means "spill blood." As a legendary war hero with a long career in Zimbabwe's government, Mujuru has been linked

JOYCE MUJURU, WHO IS PICTURED MAKING THE SYMBOLIC GESTURE OF support for ZANU-PF, is a favorite of the current ZANU-PF leadership to replace Mugabe if he retires or when he dies.

with several corruption scandals. But she has the support of ZANU-PF's leadership.

In the early 2000s, a Zimbabwean journalist wrote that MDC leader Morgan Tsvangirai "is the clear front-runner and the man most likely to be Zimbabwe's next president—if the people have any say in the matter." However, since that report, MDC has experienced a split and become weaker. Some Zimbabweans have lost hope that meaningful change can occur, and they are no longer willing to risk their safety by openly supporting MDC.

MORGAN TSVANGIRAI *(CENTER FRONT)*, **OPPOSITION PARTY MDC LEADER,** leaves court in March 2007 after being arrested and beaten for participating in a government-banned demonstration in Harare.

If a democratic leader arises in Zimbabwe after the end of the Mugabe regime, the international community is likely to help the nation recover. But because of the waste and corruption of the past, international donors will need assurances from the new government that their donated money and supplies will indeed be used for their intended purposes. Only then will they provide the resources needed to rebuild schools, hospitals, industries, and farms.

Whether a democratic leader emerges with a sound plan to restore Zimbabwe is an open question. This is partly related to the fact that the structure of Parliament itself poses a huge challenge to any candidate who advocates reform. Of the 150 seats in Parliament, the president personally selects thirty candidates, leaving 120 seats to be decided by the voters. If the president has a two-thirds majority in Parliament, he can change the constitution. Mugabe has frequently used this majority to impose his will and maintain his control. Future rulers may well do the same. In addition, Zimbabwe's ruling elite has grown rich through corruption and patronage. They have no interest in risking their privilege and status by reforming.

When Ian Smith handed over power to Robert Mugabe, Mugabe observed that he had been given "the jewel of Africa." During the years of his dictatorship, Mugabe has destroyed his jewel. He has created a government that clings to power by using force, arrests, torture, rape, and murder. Critics have compared his rule to the brutal reign of Nazi Germany's Adolf Hitler. Mugabe has challenged these critics. His response was that he would use increasingly violent methods to maintain his power; he threatened to be a "black Hitler" against his opponents. He added that if his conduct was like Hitler, "then let me be a Hitler tenfold." The world can only hope that whoever succeeds Mugabe is a humane leader with the interests of all Zimbabweans at heart.

WHO'S WHO?

MARK CHAVUNDUKA (1965-2002): Born in Harare to educated and accomplished parents, a veterinarian and a nurse, Chavunduka earned a college degree in journalism. He went to work as a reporter, then an editor, before becoming editor of an independent weekly newspaper, the *Zimbabwe Standard.* In 1999, following the publication of an article the government deemed controversial, Chavunduka and his top reporter, Ray Choto, were arrested, held for nearly two weeks, and tortured by the army. The detention sparked an international outcry and was ruled illegal by Zimbabwe's highest court. Upon his release, Chavunduka continued to publish his newspaper. Recognizing his courage, Harvard University's journalism school offered Chavunduka a fellowship in 2000, and the United States offered him political asylum. Chavunduka chose to leave Harvard and return to Harare in 2001. He died at the age of thirty-six after an unknown illness and is survived by a wife and three children. Given its high incidence in Zimbabwe, international obituaries contain speculation that he may have died of AIDS.

CHENJERAI "HITLER" HUNZVI (1949–2001): Born in rural Mashonaland, Hunzvi was the leader of Zimbabwe's National Liberation War Veterans' Association (ZNLWVA), though not actually a war veteran. He claimed to have received a medical education in Poland, where he married a Polish woman. She left him in 1992 citing abuse. Hunzvi returned to Zimbabwe in 1990 and set up a medical practice in Harare. He rose to the leadership role in ZNLWVA in 1997 and presided over increasingly violent farm invasions. He faced charges of corruption when he claimed to be 115 percent disabled from war wounds, though he had been in Europe during the war years. The ZNLWVA voted to expel him. His death at age 52 may have been due to AIDS.

THOMAS MAPFUMO (B. 1945): Born in rural Mashonaland and raised in Salisbury (Harare), Mapfumo developed a style of music, which he called "chimurenga," based on traditional Shona music and modern instruments. In 1979, during the war for independence, he was detained without charge for three months because of his music's political content. He performed at the independence day celebrations in 1980. Mapfumo was living a comfortable life in a Harare suburb, with his wife and two children, when he released an anti-Mugabe album called *Corruption* in 1989. Several years of government harassment and the threat of arrest followed, causing him to leave Zimbabwe for the United States. Mapfumo's songs still contain protests against the Mugabe regime, and he tours with his band, the Blacks Unlimited.

GRACE (MARUFU) MUGABE (B. CA. 1965): Grace Marufu Mugabe is Robert Mugabe's much younger second wife. They wed in a Catholic ceremony in 1996. Mugabe's former secretary, she was his mistress and bore him two children several years before his first wife died. She gave birth to a third child after their marriage. She is aloof from the public and spends money extravagantly. The press mocks her and the public despises her, calling her "the First Spender" and "Grabbing Grace." She had been a good student and, while still in her teens, married an air force officer, with whom she had a son. Once she became involved with Mugabe, her first husband was transferred to China and the marriage ended.

ROBERT MUGABE (B. 1924): Mugabe became the prime minister of Zimbabwe in 1980; he has been president since 1987. Educated at Kutama mission school near his birthplace, he worked as a teacher until he became involved in nationalist politics. He spent ten years (1964–1974) as a political prisoner, then led one faction in the war for independence. Since his party won the 1980 elections, he has exercised absolute power over Zimbabwe. He married Sally Hayfron in 1961; they had one child, who died. He married Grace Marufu in 1996, with whom he has three children.

SALLY (HAYFRON) MUGABE (1932–1992): Sally Hayfron Mugabe was Robert Mugabe's first wife. She was born in Ghana, where she met her future husband while she was training to be a teacher. In 1961 she spent six weeks in jail for protests against Southern Rhodesia's Smith regime. As first lady, she earned public respect through charitable works. Among her many public-spirited activities, she led the ZANU Women's League, the Zimbabwe Child Survival Movement, the Leper Society, and the Zimbabwe Women's Cooperative. Her only child died in 1966, while her husband was in prison.

JOYCE MUJURU (B. 1956): Joyce Mujuru has been the vice president of Zimbabwe since 2004. She was a commander in the war for independence. One of twelve children born to peasant farmers in rural Mashonaland, she left school and joined the war while still a teenager. Among her legendary exploits, she shot down a Rhodesian helicopter with a machine gun. After the war, she served in a series of government posts, taking time off to return to school. Among her posts were minister of Community Development, governor of central Mashonaland, minister of Information, and minister of Rural Resources and Water Development. While fighting the war, she took the name Teurai Ropa, which means "spill blood." She is married to former ZANLA commander and Zimbabwe defense chief Solomon Mujuru. They wed in 1977, when he was known as Rex Nhongo. She gave birth to two children while at war.

ABEL MUZOREWA (B. 1925): Rhodesian-born Abel Muzorewa served briefly in 1979 as prime minister of Zimbabwe-Rhodesia. He earned a master's degree in the United States in 1963, and after his return to Rhodesia became the first black bishop of the Rhodesian Methodist church. He was elected to Zimbabwe's Parliament in 1980 and ran unsuccessfully against Mugabe in later elections. In 1996 he joined forces with Edgar Tekere's opposition party to challenge Mugabe.

JOSHUA NKOMO (1917–1999): Joshua Nkomo was a leading African nationalist. He was Mugabe's main political opponent during Zimbabwe's war for independence and its early days as an independent nation. Nkomo was born at a mission in Matabeleland. His parents were Christians, and his father was a teacher and farmer. Joshua did odd jobs and worked as a carpenter, finally attending college in South Africa, where he first became interested in nationalist politics. He returned to Rhodesia in 1948 with a social work degree and worked for the national railroad as a welfare officer concerned with African workers' families. He married in 1949, but politics, prison, and war separated the couple for many years. They eventually had four children. Nkomo became president of the African National Congress in 1957. The Ian Smith regime imprisoned him for a "subversive" speech, and he remained a prisoner from 1964 to 1974. He became leader of the ZAPU party, which fought in the war for independence and opposed Mugabe's ZANU party in the 1980 elections. Mugabe set out to destroy Nkomo and his party. After being forced out of Mugabe's government and surviving an assassination attempt, Nkomo fled to Botswana in 1983. He returned to Zimbabwe and in 1987 signed an agreement to merge his party with ZANU-PF. He ceased to make public statements or talk to the press and remained in office as vice president, a largely ceremonial role, until his death.

CECIL JOHN RHODES (1853–1902): Cecil John Rhodes founded the British South Africa Company. Born in England, he was the son of a clergyman. He emigrated to the Cape province (in present-day South Africa) in 1870. Founder of the DeBeers diamond mining company, he became governor of the Cape in 1890. As part of his plan to build a British-controlled railroad running the length of Africa, he formed the British South Africa Company and sent the Pioneer Column of soldiers and settlers northward into present-day Zimbabwe. His will directed that his fortune be used to create the Rhodes Scholarships.

NDABANINGI SITHOLE (1920–2000): Born in Rhodesia, Ndabaningi Sithole was the founder of the ZANU party; he was displaced by Mugabe. A Methodist minister with a doctorate in theology, he was jailed along with Mugabe from 1964 to 1974. Accused of plotting to kill Ian Smith, he renounced violence, and this gave Mugabe the pretext to maneuver him out of power. Since Sithole was Ndebele and Mugabe was Shona, the party split along tribal lines, and Sithole founded a new party that he called ZANU-Ndonga. He joined forces with Abel Muzorewa in 1979 but went into exile in the United States in 1983. He returned in 1992 to oppose Mugabe again and was elected to Parliament in 1995. In revenge Mugabe had him arrested and charged with plotting to kill him. He was banned from taking his seat in Parliament. After two years, the charges were dropped because of his failing health. He died in the United States, survived by his wife and five children.

IAN SMITH (B. 1919): Ian Smith served as the prime minister of white-ruled Rhodesia from 1964 until 1979. Born in Rhodesia, he became a fighter pilot in the country's air force during World War II. As prime minister, he declared Rhodesia's independence from Great Britain in 1965 in order to retain power in the hands of the white minority. He remained active in Zimbabwean politics and continued to criticize Mugabe in spite of ongoing harassment. He married and had one son, but his wife and son have both died. He lives in South Africa.

EDGAR TEKERE (B. 1937): Edgar Tekere is a founding member of ZANU and a Mugabe loyalist who later became a major opponent. Tekere fought in the war for independence and occupied a cabinet post in Mugabe's government. While pursuing members of Joshua Nkomo's ZAPU party, Tekere killed a white farmer. He was charged with murder but was acquitted. He left Mugabe's government but remained part of the ZANU leadership and began criticizing the government. In 1989 he founded the opposition party Zimbabwe Unity Movement (ZUM) and ran unsuccessfully against Mugabe in the 1990 elections. He has since rejoined ZANU-PF.

MORGAN TSVANGIRAI (B. 1952): Morgan Tsvangirai is a political opponent of Mugabe and the founder of the major opposition party, Movement for Democratic Change (MDC). Born in central Zimbabwe, he was the eldest of nine children and left school at age sixteen. He worked in a mine and a factory and eventually rose to leadership of the Zimbabwe Congress of Trade Unions. He launched the Movement for Democratic Change in 1999 to oppose Mugabe's regime. In Zimbabwe's earliest days as an independent nation, Tsvangirai had idolized Mugabe and later said, "I think I would have died for the man." As leader of the opposition party, he has survived three assassination attempts and faced numerous charges of treason. He is married with six children.

TIMELINE

1200–1450   The stone fortress known as the Great Zimbabwe is built and inhabited by Africans.

1511   Portuguese explorer Antonio Fernandes is the first European to set foot in what later becomes Zimbabwe.

1850   As European nations compete to colonize Africa, the Age of Imperialism begins. It lasts until 1914.

1888   The Ndebele chief Lobengula signs the Rudd Concession, granting extensive rights to the British.

1889   Cecil Rhodes establishes the British South Africa Company.

1890   The British South Africa Company's Pioneer Column enters Lobengula's territory.

1896   The Ndebele and the Shona join forces against the whites in the First Chimurenga.

1897   The British squash all native resistance to their presence in Southern Rhodesia.

1923   Southern Rhodesia becomes a British colony.

1924   Robert Mugabe is born on February 21.

1945   World War II ends. Soon after, American political leaders pressure British and other European colonial powers to grant independence to their colonies.

1964–1974   Robert Mugabe and other nationalist leaders are political prisoners of Ian Smith's regime.

1965   Ian Smith declares white-ruled Rhodesia independent from Great Britain in order to avoid giving Africans political power.

1966–1979   African nationalists fight for control of Rhodesia in the Second Chimurenga.

1979 African leaders meet at the Lancaster House Conference in London to forge an agreement to institute black majority rule.

1980 Zimbabwe becomes an independent nation; Robert Mugabe is inaugurated as prime minister.

1983–1987 Mugabe unleashes the Fifth Brigade against Matabeleland in a terror campaign that kills thousands.

1987 With the signing of the Unity Accord, Mugabe's ZANU-PF party absorbs Joshua Nkomo's ZAPU party, effectively making Zimbabwe a one-party state.

1998 Mugabe sends Zimbabwean troops to fight in the Congo, at the cost of $1 million a day, further crippling the nation's economy.

1999 Morgan Tsvangirai forms a new opposition party, Movement for Democratic Change (MDC), to challenge Mugabe. Mugabe unleashes a reign of terror against MDC supporters.

2000 Mugabe receives his first political defeat at the hands of Zimbabwe's voters when they reject his proposed new constitution. He blames the white population and steps up the confiscation of white-owned farms.

2002 After a campaign to intimidate voters, Mugabe wins reelection as president, defeating Morgan Tsvangirai of the MDC.

2003 Morgan Tsvangirai is charged with treason.

2005 Mugabe authorizes Operation Murambatsvina to demolish homes in the most poverty-stricken areas of Zimbabwe's cities.

2006 ZANU-PF postpones the 2008 presidential election until 2010. Operation Murambatsvina resumes for one month in May.

2007 Based in part on reports from Human Rights Watch, Amnesty International, Reporters Without Borders, and the U.S. State Department, *Parade* magazine names Mugabe one of the world's ten worst dictators.

GLOSSARY

apartheid: a political policy in which people of different races are kept apart from each other

black market: informal or illegal sale and purchase of goods outside the regular economy

bush: woodland; back country

chaff: seed coverings and other debris that are separated from the seed during threshing; something considered worthless

conventional warfare: armed conflict that employs nonnuclear weapons

coup: the violent overthrow of an existing government by a small group

dissident: one who disagrees with an established political or religious system, organization, or belief

Fifth Brigade: a special army force used by Mugabe and ZANU-PF to squash the rival party, ZAPU, by terrorizing supporters in Matabeleland

guerrilla warfare: conflict engaged in primarily by those (called guerrillas) who comprise independent units that carry out harassment and sabotage

HIV: human immunodeficiency virus, the cause of AIDS (acquired immunodeficiency syndrome), which is transmitted through sexual contact or sharing needles, incurable, and often fatal

imperialism: the policy, practice, or advocacy of extending a nation's power, especially by acquiring land or by gaining control over the political or economic life of other areas

inflation: a continuing rise in the general price level usually attributed to an increase in the volume of money and credit relative to available goods and services

Mashonaland: the homeland of the Shona people

Matabeleland: the homeland of the Ndebele people

MDC: Movement for Democratic Change; an opposition party founded in 1999 by Morgan Tsvangirai

nationalism: support of national independence

nationalize: to place a privately owned business or property under ownership and control of the national government

Ndebele: the minority native tribe comprising about 20 percent of Zimbabwe's population

Operation Murambatsvina: a campaign of the 2000s directed against the country's poor people

pandemic: the outbreak of a disease that occurs over a wide geographic area and affects an exceptionally high proportion of the population

police state: a society characterized by repressive governmental control of political, economic, and social life usually by an arbitrary exercise of power by police and especially secret police in place of the regular operation of government

protectorate: a political unit or territory that is under the political control of another power or state

sanctions: economic or military restrictions enacted, usually by several nations at once, to force another nation to stop violating international law

Shona: the majority native tribe of Zimbabwe, to which Mugabe belongs, comprising about 75 percent of the nation's population

subjugated: conquered, controlled, and governed by a superior power

township: an urban area where nonwhites live

treason: the offense of attempting to overthrow the government of the state to which the offender owes allegiance, or to kill or personally injure the head of state or government

warlord: a military commander exercising power by force, usually in a limited area

Western: of or relating to the noncommunist countries of North America and Europe

ZANLA: Zimbabwe African National Liberation Army; the military wing of ZANU

ZANU: Zimbabwe African National Union; the Shona-based party that fought to overthrow the white government of Rhodesia

ZANU-PF: Zimbabwe African National Union-Patriotic Front; Mugabe's ruling party, as it was renamed once ZANU absorbed ZAPU

ZAPU: Zimbabwe African People's Union; led by Joshua Nkomo, one of the two parties that fought for Zimbabwean independence; dissolved in 1987

ZIPRA: Zimbabwe People's Revolutionary Army; the military wing of ZAPU

BIBLIOGRAPHY

Author interview with Beth Wilkins, Lexington, Virginia, June 29, 2006.

Blair, David. *Degrees in Violence: Robert Mugabe and the Struggle for Power in Zimbabwe.* New York: Continuum, 2002.

Chan, Stephen. *Robert Mugabe: A Life of Power and Violence.* Ann Arbor, MI: University of Michigan Press, 2003.

Hill, Geoff. *What Happens after Mugabe? Can Zimbabwe Rise from the Ashes?* Cape Town, South Africa: Zebra Press, 2005.

Meldrum, Andrew. *Where We Have Hope: A Memoir of Zimbabwe.* New York: Atlantic Monthly Press, 2004.

Meredith, Martin. *The Fate of Africa: From the Hopes of Freedom to the Heart of Despair: A History of 50 Years of Independence.* New York: Public Affairs, 2005.

Nkomo, Joshua. *Nkomo: The Story of My Life.* London: Methuen, 1984.

Owomoyela, Oyekan. *Culture and Customs of Zimbabwe.* Westport, CT: Greenwood Press, 2002.

Sayce, Katherine, ed. *Tabex Encyclopedia Zimbabwe.* Harare, Zimbabwe: Quest Publishing Ltd., 1987.

Smith, Ian. *The Great Betrayal: The Memoirs of Ian Douglas Smith.* London: Blake Publishing Ltd., 1997.

Staunton, Irene, ed. *Mothers of the Revolution: The War Experiences of Thirty Zimbabwean Women.* Bloomington, IN: Indiana University Press, 1991.

Weiss, Ruth. *Zimbabwe and the New Elite.* London: British Academic Press, 1994.

FURTHER READING, WEBSITES, AND BLOGS

BOOKS

Buckle, Catherine. *African Tears: The Zimbabwe Land Invasions.* Weltevredenpark, South Africa: Covos Day Books, 2001. The author, a white farmer evicted from her property, regularly posts reports from Zimbabwe on her website (see p. 153). Some of her reports have been published in this book, as well as the sequel, *Beyond Tears.*

DiPiazza, Francesca. *Zimbabwe in Pictures.* Minneapolis: Twenty-First Century Books, 2005. This title in the Visual Geography Series enhances readers' knowledge of Zimbabwe's geography, people, history, government, economy, and cultural life.

Fuller, Alexandra. *Don't Let's Go to the Dogs Tonight: An African Childhood.* New York: Random House, 2001. Born in England in 1969, the author spent much of her childhood on farms in Zimbabwe.

Godwin, Peter. *Mukiwa: A White Boy in Africa.* New York: Atlantic Monthly Press, 1996. Godwin writes with affection of being a boy in Zimbabwe's Eastern Highlands. As he grows up, he witnesses the violence and confusion of the collapsing colony. Though he supported independence, he found himself fulfilling his national service as a policeman in Matabeleland. Later, as a journalist, he covered the Fifth Brigade atrocities there.

Hill, Geoff. *The Battle for Zimbabwe: The Final Countdown.* Cape Town, South Africa: Struik Publishers, 2005. The author explores life for those in ZANU-PF and MDC and considers Zimbabwe's future challenge to rebuild the country when Mugabe's regime finally ends.

Lessing, Doris. *African Laughter: Four Visits to Zimbabwe.* New York: Harper Perennial, 1993. Lessing, who grew up in Rhodesia, describes four visits to Zimbabwe after independence.

WEBSITES AND BLOGS

African Tears

> http://www.africantears.netfirms.com
>
> Catherine Buckle, a white farmer evicted from the property she had purchased after independence, regularly posts reports from Zimbabwe, where she still resides.

New Zimbabwe

> http://www.newzimbabwe.com
>
> This news website is dedicated to freedom of expression. It hosts on-line forums with postings by people inside and outside of Zimbabwe.

The Zimbabwean

> http://www.thezimbabwean.co.uk
>
> This independent online and print newspaper, created by and for Zimbabweans in exile, is edited by Wilf Mbanga, founder of the *Daily News*, which Zimbabwean authorities closed down in 2003.

Zimbabwean Pundit

> http://www.zimpundit.blogspot.com
>
> The Zimbabwean Pundit contains articles posted from Zimbabwe by a Zimbabwean. The site also provides links to other blogs from Zimbabwe.

Zimbabwe Situation

> http://www.zimbabwesituation.com
>
> This independent site provides daily news updates from Zimbabwe and links to organizations working to help Zimbabwe's oppressed people.

Zvakwana

> http://www.zvakwana.com
>
> *Zvakwana*, the name of this online newsletter, means "enough is enough." Its stated purpose is to inform Zimbabweans about the news and promote activism.

SOURCE NOTES

8 "Zimbabwe's Independence," 2006, http://www.info-ghana.com/zimbabwe's_independence.htm (June 2006).

9 Ibid.

10 Ibid.

23 "The Atlantic Charter," *The Annals of America*, vol. 16 (Chicago: Encyclopaedia Britannica, Inc., 1976), 89–90.

36 David Blair, *Degrees in Violence: Robert Mugabe and the Struggle for Power in Zimbabwe* (New York: Continuum, 2002), 21.

46 Irene Staunton, ed., *Mothers of the Revolution: The War Experiences of Thirty Zimbabwean Women* (Bloomington: Indiana University Press, 1991), 194–195.

46 Ruth Weiss, *Zimbabwe and the New Elite* (London: British Academic Press, 1994), 56.

46 Staunton, *Mothers of the Revolution*, 156–157.

47 Ian Smith, *The Great Betrayal: The Memoirs of Ian Douglas Smith* (London: Blake Publishing Ltd., 1997), 358.

47 Staunton, *Mothers of the Revolution*, 234–235.

48 David Blair, *Degrees in Violence*, 11.

51 Ibid., 14.

53 Geoff Hill, *What Happens after Mugabe? Can Zimbabwe Rise from the Ashes?* (Cape Town, South Africa: Zebra Press, 2005), 8.

59 Martin Meredith, *The Fate of Africa: From the Hopes of Freedom to the Heart of Despair: A History of 50 Years of Independence* (New York: Public Affairs, 2005), 620.

60 Joshua Nkomo, *Nkomo: The Story of My Life* (London: Methuen, 1984), 2.

60 Meredith, *The Fate of Africa*, 623.

61 Nkomo, *Nkomo: The Story of My Life*, 237.

61–62 Meredith, *The Fate of Africa,*
623.

63 Ibid., 625.

66 Smith, *The Great Betrayal,*
380.

69 Meredith, *The Fate of Africa,*
630.

74 Stephen Chan, *Robert
Mugabe: A Life of Power and
Violence* (Ann Arbor:
University of Michigan
Press, 2003), 145.

78 "Commonwealth Observer
Group's Preliminary Report
on Zimbabwean Presidential
Elections," March 14, 2002,
http://www.afrol.com/
Countries/Zimbabwe/
documents/commonw
_election_group.htm (June
2006).

79 "Zimbabwe: Running Down
a Tyrant," *Amnesty
International Canada,* July
2002, http://www.amnesty
.ca/Zimbabwe/Coltart
_interview.php (January
2007).

80 "Vote ZANU-PF or Starve:
Zimbabwe August to
October 2002," *Physicians
for Human Rights,* Denmark,

November 20, 2002,
http://www.swradioafrica
.com/Documents/Physicians
.htm (January 2007).

85 Alison Jones Webb, "Torture
Chronicles," *Colby* 94:3 (Fall
2005), 37.

85 Human Rights Watch,
"Zimbabwe Denies
Protections and Assistance
to the Evicted," *Human
Rights News,* December 1,
2005, http://hrw.org/
english/docs/2005/12/01/
zimbab12111.htm (May
2006).

90 "'I haven't lost hope':
Personal Account of the
Daily News editor Samuel
Sipepa Nkomo," *Reporters
Without Borders,* August 19,
2005, http://www.rsf.org/
article.php3?id_article
=14738 (May 2006).

91 Mark Glaser, "Zimbabwe's
Daily News Fights Closure
with Online Publication,"
Online Journalism Review,
October 10, 2003, http://
www.ojr.org/ojr/glaser/
1066860746.php (May
2006).

92 Human Rights Watch, "Zimbabwe: Crackdown on the Press Intensifies," *Human Rights News,* February 9, 2006 http://hrw.org/english/docs/2006/02/08/zimbab12632.htm (May 2006).

95 Mark Chavunduka, "Imprisonment and Torture of Journalists in Zimbabwe," *The Nieman Foundation for Journalism at Harvard University* 54:3 (Fall 2000), 82.

99 Marian L. Tupy, "Bureaucratic Heart of Darkness," *The Washington Times* (April 16, 2006).

100 allAfrica.com, "Zimbabwe: Critics Warn of Catastrophe if Mugabe 'Steals' Election," allAfrica.com, February 3, 2002, http://allafrica.com/stories/200202030024.html (June 2006).

101 "Zimbabwe Committed to Fighting Corruption," *People's Daily Online,* December 18, 2005, http://english.people.com.cn/200512/18/eng20051218_228913.html (June 2006).

105 "Zimbabwe's Independence," 2006, http://www.info-ghana.com/zimbabwe's _ independence.htm (June 2006).

108 Omen Muza, "Zimbabwe: A Case of Music Censorship Before and After Independence," *Freemuse: Freedom of Musical Expression,* May 12, 2005, http://www.freemuse.org/sw9326.asp (May 2006).

111 Webb, "Torture Chronicles," 37.

112 Amnesty International, "Report 2005: Zimbabwe," 2005, http://web.amnesty.org/report2005/zwe-summary-eng (June 2006).

114 Staunton, *Mothers of the Revolution,* 195.

115 Ibid., 112.

115 Dzikamai Chiyausiku, "Zimbabwe: Harsh Realities of Daily Life," *ReliefWeb,* October 21, 2005, http://www.reliefweb.int/rw/RWB.NSF/db900SID/RMOI-6HG57X?OpenDocument&rc=1&emid=ACOS-635PKL (June 2006).

116 Staunton, *Mothers of the Revolution,* 155.

119 Yaroslav Trofimov, "Zimbabwe's Opposition Falters," *Wall Street Journal* (November 30, 2005), A17.

120 Staunton, *Mothers of the Revolution*, 248.

122 Dzikamai Chiyausiku, "Zimbabwe: Harsh Realities of Daily Life."

122 Ibid.

123 Saul Dambaza, "Zimbabwe: School Fees Hike Fuels Dropout Rate," *Africa Reports, Institute for War and Peace Reporting,* June 27, 2006, http://iwpr.net/?p=acr&s =f&o=321869&apc_state =heniacr2006 (July 2006).

125 Andrew Meldrum, *Where We Have Hope: A Memoir of Zimbabwe* (New York: Atlantic Monthly Press, 2004), 145.

129 "To Boost Economy, Some Africans Woo White Farmers," *Wall Street Journal* (November 17, 2005), A1.

130 Hill, *What Happens After Mugabe?*, 20.

134 Trofimov, "Zimbabwe's Opposition Falters," A16.

134 allAfrica.com, "Zimbabwe: Critics Warn of Catastrophe if Mugabe 'Steals' Election," *allAfrica.com*, February 3, 2002, http://allafrica .com/stories/200202030024 .html (June 2006).

137 Dumisani Muleya, "Tsvangirai is the Pick of a Poor Crop of Candidates," *The Zimbabwe Situation,* May 25, 2003, <http://www .zimbabwesituation.com/ May 25_2003.html#link3 (June 2006).

139 Meredith, *The Fate of Africa,* 646.

145 Blair, *Degrees in Violence,* 38.

INDEX

African independence, 25, 26–27, 39
AIDS, 10, 83, 130–131, 133, 140
army, 52, 57, 59, 64, 69, 72, 81, 100,
    112; veterans, 55, 57, 72, 75, 77,
    120, 140

censorship, 24, 74, 88–92, 95, 96,
    106, 108–109, 111
Chavunduka, Mark, 95, 100, 140
colonialism, 8, 15–17, 20–22, 25,
    26–27, 102–103
Commonwealth, 78, 79, 102–103
Communism, 40, 48, 58, 102;
    Mugabe and, 48, 52, 58, 65–66,
    123
Congo, war in, 73, 100, 104
Constitution, 65, 68, 71, 73, 82, 92–93,
    94, 136; referendum on, 74
corruption, 100–101, 124, 134

daily life, 9–10, 68, 80, 87, 113, 117,
    119, 122–123, 132, 133

economy, 48, 55, 58–59, 64, 65,
    113–119, 123; agriculture, 9, 47,
    58, 66, 77, 115–116, 123;
    collapse of, 9–10, 81, 124;
    inflation, 66, 68, 72, 81;
    unemployment, 73, 99, 115, 119,
    121
education, 9–10, 21, 22, 32, 54, 66,
    72, 119–123
elections, 44, 48–51, 63, 68, 74, 78,
    82, 93; corrupt, 70–71, 78–79,
    81, 111, 134
emigration, 52, 82, 86, 106, 117, 118,
    128–129
ethnic groups, 12–15, 18–19, 29, 35,
    86. See also Ndebele; Shona

farms, 6–7, 9, 24, 47, 54, 58, 81, 87,
    114–116. See also economy; land
food, 79–80, 81, 87, 107, 115, 122

foreign relations, 26, 28, 29, 48, 52,
    79, 96, 102–108

Great Britain, 16, 23, 25, 26, 31, 44,
    46, 50, 128
guerrillas, 28, 29, 31, 39, 42–43, 59
gukurahundi, 60–63, 64

health, 10, 32–33, 69, 80, 129–131,
    133
history, pre-independence, 6, 12–31,
    114–115, 116, 119, 129
homelessness, 10, 83, 84, 85
human rights groups, 8, 80–81, 85,
    92, 95, 108
Hunzvi, Chenjerai, 75, 77, 140

independence, 6, 8, 31, 45–52, 110,
    113, 117, 129–130
international aid, 54, 69, 79, 80–81,
    85, 98, 103, 105, 120, 131, 138
Internet, 90–92, 108

labor unions, 66, 71
Lancaster House Agreement, 45–47,
    94, 113
land, 19, 56; ownership, 18, 22, 24,
    56, 68, 69–70, 99–100; reform, 9,
    46–47, 68–69, 99–100; seizures,
    9, 68–69, 72, 75, 77, 99–100,
    125–129, 140
laws and courts, 24, 36, 58, 60, 65,
    75, 79, 87, 90, 92, 94, 111

Matabeleland, 17, 60–63, 64
Matonga, Bright, 98–99
MDC, 73, 77, 79, 82, 135–136, 137,
    145
media, 55, 74, 86–87, 88–92, 95, 106,
    140
Mozambique, 29, 38–39, 40, 45, 64,
    65, 129
Mugabe, Grace, 71–72, 141

Mugabe, Robert, 141; army leader, 40–41, 45; becomes president, 65, 93; becomes prime minister, 6–7, 31, 50–53, 93; childhood, 17, 32; education, 32, 33, 37; gains absolute power, 58–59, 64–66, 93; lifestyle, 69, 70, 72, 124, 128; marriages, 34, 71, 141; in prison, 36, 37, 39; promises reconciliation, 7, 51–53, 54, 117; promotes race hatred, 41, 48, 69, 72, 74–75; religion, 17, 32, 33; teacher, 34; successor to, 136–139
Mugabe, Sally, 34–35, 37, 71, 142
Mujuru, Joyce, 136–137, 142
music, 108, 109, 141
Muzorewa, Abel, 44, 45, 142

nationalism, African, 23, 25, 28, 34, 39, 105; in Rhodesia, 6, 8, 10, 36, 37
Ndebele, 14–15, 19, 20, 28, 49, 86
Nkomo, Joshua, 28, 29, 34, 36, 39, 40, 51–52, 59, 143; relations with Mugabe, 49–50, 58, 59–60, 64

Operation Murambatsvina, 10, 83, 84, 85, 121–122
opposition, 66–68, 69, 70–71, 72, 73, 77–78, 81, 90–92, 109, 130, 134. See also MDC

Parliament, 48, 49–50, 63, 82, 93; Mugabe controls, 65, 67–68, 70, 77–78, 82, 138–139
patronage, 66, 99–101, 134
police, 19, 52, 62, 63, 81, 112, 122
poor people, 10, 83–85, 119, 121–122, 123
propaganda, 55, 96, 97–99

Rhodes, Cecil, 16, 17, 20, 143
Rhodesia, 6, 25–26, 28–29, 30, 31, 36, 88

Shona, 12–13, 14–15, 18–19, 20, 28, 49, 86
Sithole, Ndabaningi, 36, 37, 38, 39, 44, 144
Smith, Ian, 25, 27, 28, 29, 31, 36, 37, 44–47, 88, 108, 144; post-independence, 52, 54–55, 58, 65
South Africa, 14, 18, 26, 28, 39, 50, 64, 103, 106, 143; relations with Zimbabwe, 103, 105

Tekere, Edgar, 66–67, 68, 144
terror and intimidation, 42–43, 50, 58, 60–63, 67, 77, 78, 82, 111, 112, 130
Tsvangirai, Morgan, 66, 73, 77, 78, 79, 137, 138, 145

war of independence, 6, 8–9, 28–29, 30, 39–48, 130, 136, 141, 142, 143
white Rhodesians, 22–23, 24, 25, 28, 30, 46–47, 50, 51, 52
white Zimbabweans, 58, 65, 76, 86, 117–118, 124–125, 128–129. See also land: seizures

youth militias, 62, 63, 78, 80, 81, 112, 130; green bombers, 82

ZANU, 28–29, 35, 37–38, 40–41, 49–51, 57, 58; army of, 40; Fifth Brigade of, 59, 60; Shona support, 49, 59
ZANU–PF, 64, 74, 93, 112, 136–137; privileges of, 100, 101, 107
ZAPU, 28–29, 35, 49–51, 63–65; army of, 40, 59; Ndebele support, 49, 60
Zimbabwe: climate, 56; government structure, 93; location and size, 11, 12; names of, 6, 17, 20, 30, 45; population, 86, 114, 118, 130
ZUM, 67, 68, 144

PHOTO ACKNOWLEDGMENTS

AUTHOR BIOGRAPHIES

James R. Arnold has written more than twenty-five political history and military history books on topics ranging from the Napoleonic Wars to the origins of the American involvement in Vietnam. His published titles include *Crisis on the Danube: Napoleon's Austrian Campaign of 1809* and *Grant Wins the War: Decision at Vicksburg*. Arnold's essays have appeared in *The Journal of Military History; Reader's Guide to Military History; Navy History; Northern Virginia Heritage; Army;* and the *Journal of the Society for Army Historical Research*.

Roberta Wiener has coauthored numerous works of history with James R. Arnold and contributed to numerous works of juvenile history, including a thirteen-volume history of American colonies.

Arnold and Wiener are currently providing historical content and analysis for ABC-Clio's website *The United States at War: Understanding Conflict and Society*, and editorial services to the Virginia Military Institute's John A. Adams Center for Military History and Strategic Analysis, and for *International Perspectives*. They are also working on a history of counterinsurgency.